Made with Meaning

God's purpose for bodies and the language they speak

David Tipton

AI

0101

Made with Meaning
God's Purpose for Bodies and the Language They Speak
by David Tipton

ISBN: 978-1-954509-04-7

Printed in the USA.

Published by visionrun.com

To John Paul II and John Piper, whom I hope to meet, and perhaps even introduce to each other in the resurrection.

Acknowledgments

First, to my dear wife Alison. Her edits and suggestions proved invaluable on many occasions, from finding grammatical errors to forcing me to clarify my thoughts, she did it often while nursing our fourth child. She also has put up with me saying "[Fill in the blank] says..." so many times that she's ready to scream.

Second, Debbie Patrick at Vision Run. Her experience in publishing and writing helped me get unstuck and provided a crucial, practical way forward. As her line editor, Elisabeth Quayle's eye for detail was also invaluable.

Third, two people from the Diocese of Knoxville were very helpful. Lt. Col. Paul Simoneau (Ret. USMC), the Director of the Office of Justice and Peace for the Diocese of Knoxville. He introduced me to Catholic teaching beyond what I had. Also, Sister Anna Marie McGuan (RSM) helped me get through a tough spot of chapter six, which proved devilishly difficult to write.

Contents

Introduction 9

Chapter 1
   How Did We Get to This Point? 15

Chapter 2
   As It Was in the Beginning 27

Chapter 3
   Not How Things are Supposed to Be 45

Chapter4
   Managing the Fallenness 69

Chapter 5
   What God Has Joined Together,
   Let Not Man Put Asunder 89

Chapter 6
   "More Human Than Human" or Not at All 111

Chapter 7
   World Without End 133

About the Author 152

Introduction

This work owes a great deal to three people.

First, John Paul II. My own thoughts on marriage and sexuality closely tracked with Rome's through the years, even on divorce. (I've modified my position slightly — see chapter 4 for further details.) I had more in common with them than I realized just by being raised in an unusually conservative church on such matters. My own forays into Catholic sexual teaching were sparked by a Protestant couple who openly stated that they used natural family planning. The husband was an ex-Catholic, and it got me wondering what the church said and why, especially to draw an ex-member back to one of the most openly reviled areas of Catholic teaching, at least in the USA. I picked up *Humanae Vitae* and was shocked by what I read. This wasn't an imperious, because-I-said-so decree. This was a carefully reasoned, thoughtfully presented, and calm declaration. It also anticipated China's one-child policy, which reinforced its impression on me.

Being raised Protestant, I didn't have the background teaching and culture to fully understand Paul VI's arguments. One of my misconceptions was that *Humanae Vitae* was mainly about contraception. It's really about much more than that, but all the furor around the encyclical obscured some of what Paul VI was teaching. One of his successors, John Paul II, had been working for years to expand on the encyclical's teaching and explain how it applied to much more than just contraception. Shortly after his election as pope in 1978, he started devoting his weekly Papal Audiences to the subject. These audiences were collected into a work commonly called the *Theology of the Body*, which had recently been reprinted in an updated English translation. It was highly recommended, and I happened to find a pristine copy at our local used bookstore. Even though it was 600 pages (that includes the 100-page introduction), I promised myself I would read it through.[1]

That took me four years and three attempts. Part of the reason was John Paul's dense philosophical language, which I was unfamiliar with. Another part was a deep encounter with Catholic theology, and sorting that out in my own head, a process which is still playing out somewhat. A final part was the sheer volume of the work. However, when I finished, I found my worldview permanently changed. I looked at many of the questions about bodiliness and sexuality facing the West through the *Theology of the Body* lens. I found myself with new insights to understand what was happening and why, and I wanted to encourage my Protestant brethren to come with me.

There was a problem; *Theology of the Body* is not a work that most people will just sit down and read. Unlike some of John Paul II's encyclicals, the language of *Theology of the Body* is dense and difficult to understand unless one either has philosophical

---

1   The version referenced in this book is *Man and Woman He Created Them (A Theology of the Body)*, translated by Michael Waldstein (Pauline Books and Media, Boston, MA, 2006). This will be referred to as *Theology of the Body* throughout the rest of the book.

training or the time to work through his arguments. There is now a growing body of Catholic work that attempts to translate John Paul's thought to a man-on-the-street level.[2] That still left me with a problem. Even though there was a great deal of truth in *Theology of the Body*, I didn't agree with significant portions of the teaching, especially the assertion that marriage was a sacrament. I didn't have a book that I felt comfortable giving to people without qualifications. Could *Theology of the Body* be translated to a Protestant milieu? Many Catholics would argue, "No." The more I thought about it, the more I got the feeling that the answer was "Maybe..."

John Piper has probably influenced me more than any single writer. I didn't discover him until I was in my mid-twenties. Sadly, my theological education had been woefully neglected, and my mentor at the time introduced me to many authors, including Piper. I thought *Desiring God* was okay, but it was his next work, *The Pleasures of God*, that opened my eyes to the riches of Christ. I could go on — *Future Grace, A Godward Life, Don't Waste Your Life*, and sermons and articles too many to count. Like him or loathe him, one thing about John Piper is not up for dispute — he seems to be a happy man. That happiness (he would probably prefer the word "joyful") flows out of his basic premise that "God is most glorified in us when we are most satisfied in him."[3] I wanted — and still want — that joy. Where to get it? Simple — soak in the word of God. Stew in it. In a manner of speaking, eat it (Eze. 2:1-3; Rev. 10:9-10). Be relentlessly biblical. One of his lasting contributions to my life was to gently point out that, contrary to what I thought I was

---

2   For my Catholic readers, please see *Theology of the Body for Beginners* by Christopher West. In my opinion, this is the best one that I've encountered so far.
3   John Piper, *Desiring God, 10th Anniversary Expanded Edition* (Multinomah Press, Sisters, OR, 1996), pg. 50.

doing, I was allowing the culture to dictate how I understood the Scriptures, instead of going to the Scriptures to understand the culture.

I mentioned above that my views on marriage had altered slightly — with emphasis on slightly — and John Piper is responsible. This will be detailed further in chapter 4, but for the moment, let's just say that he was more biblical than I was, and for that, I am grateful.

Finally, Father Stephen Freeman, rector emeritus of St. Anne Orthodox Church, and blogger extraordinaire. Father Stephen's blog, Glory to God for All Things,[4] consistently challenges a Western view of the world, Western Christianity, and modernity in general. Father Stephen began his ministerial life as an Episcopal priest and later converted to Eastern Orthodoxy.

If you ever read him, prepare to be made very uncomfortable. You'll notice that the idea of "icon" runs throughout this book. He — and Eastern Orthodoxy — are responsible. Most of our lives are iconographic, and we far too often either mistake icons for the real thing or deny that there is a real thing and devalue the icon in the process.

Before you start, be aware that this book, while I welcome non-Christians who may read it, is not written for non-Christians. This book is a call for the church in my homeland (the USA) to shake off its torpor, repent, and live as we have been commanded. St. Paul's dictum that "sexual immorality... must not even be named among you" (Eph. 5:3) leaves many of us short. By our lives, we're saying that the short-term pleasures of sin are better than the eternal riches of Christ

4   blogs.ancientfaith.com/glory2godforallthings

(see Heb. 11:25-26; 2 Tim. 4). We are trading valuable riches for filth.

This is also a subject on which volumes can and have been written. I am not a trained philosopher, and more in-depth treatments of this subject are available for those who are unsatisfied with what I've done in this work. This book is intended as an introductory primer for those who have never even heard of *Theology of the Body* and is written by a Protestant primarily for Protestants. It also addresses questions that John Paul II did not, most notably chapters 6 and 7.

Why has the church lost its influence in the culture? While this is a complex question, one of the answers is undoubtedly that we tried to give people the same thing that they found in the world, and when "seekers" discovered that the world did it better, they tuned us out. For over 100 years, we've reaped the bitter fruit of our error. As is frequently the case, we lost the battle years before we even started fighting.

This book is a call to get serious. We need to repent of our fornications and get over our reticence to discuss sexual matters in the church. We think we're on the battlefield fighting the good fight, when we're really just playing around on the firing range.

"When Jesus Christ calls a man, he bids him come and die."[5] This book is a call to my fellow Protestants to die to the sexual zeitgeist and find true life. It is a call to abandon the emptiness of this passing evil age and find fullness in Christ and obedience to him — no matter how difficult it may seem.

5   Deitrich Bonhoffer, *The Cost of Discipleship* (Touchstone, NY, NY, 1995), pg. 89.

Chapter 1

How Did We Get to This Point?

This might seem like a book about sex, but it's not. It's a book about human bodies. This book is ultimately about what bodies mean, why it matters, and how that should work out in practice. Yes, sex shows up a lot, but it shows up a lot because sex — in both senses — matters a lot. It's at the heart of many questions that our society is asking:

"Is there something better than hooking up, and if so, what?"

"My neighbors are homosexual. How can I be a good neighbor to them?"

"What do I tell my son when his friends show him a *Sports Illustrated* swimsuit issue?"

"My daughter's friend is "transitioning," and now my daughter's asking questions. What do I say?"

While some of these problems are as old as human sin itself, there are brand new spins to others. Once, the Western church dealt with these issues from a position of cultural strength, but no more. In a blink of an eye, the ground has shifted under our feet. As recently as the early 1980s, the pervasiveness of pornography, the hyper-sexualization of popular culture, the idea that two men could be married, the idea that biological men could be women and vice versa, and the widespread, outright, petulant defiance that we now see from abortionists would have been unthinkable.

I think that what shocked so many of us was the speed with which formerly unthinkable taboos became the demanded norms. While mass media undoubtedly had an accelerating effect, the collapse of the Christian-informed ethic on marriage and family was well underway before cable, Twitter, and the internet. Some of us saw it coming,[1] but I'm not sure if anyone anticipated the speed at which orthodox Christian teaching on marriage, sexuality, and even what it means to be human, went from being considered mildly irritating to a borderline thought crime. While much has been and will continue to be written about the causes of our current situation, the focus of this book is on what the church should do next.

What has the church been doing so far? It's not like we haven't been active. We've tried marriage seminars, purity rings, prayer walks at abortion clinics, accountability groups, and the like. It hasn't made a dent in our divorce, abortion, or pornography usage rates. We have made the typical mistake of conflating effects with causes. Simply yelling, "Stop that!" hasn't worked, either. In a certain sense, neither has proclaiming biblical ethics, because we proved by our actions that we didn't believe them in the first place. While we do need clarion calls from pulpits to return to biblical sexual ethics as the only sure way to achieve human sexual flourishing, we find that people aren't listening to the Scriptures. When we behave like the world, and thus show

---

1   Namely, C.S. Lewis and Francis Schaeffer, especially Schaeffer. For Lewis, I recommend *The Abolition of Man*. For Schaeffer, *The God Who is There* and *A Christian Manifesto* are terrifying in their prescience.

that we love what it loves in very similar ways, why should non-believers listen? Behavior modification isn't enough though; "My people are destroyed for lack of knowledge" (Hos. 4:6), and "a good man out of the good treasure of his heart bringeth forth good things" (Mat. 12:35, KJV). The solution is not to stop preaching the truth, but to preach it more thoroughly and to apply the Scriptures to the root cause, not just the symptoms.

So what is the root cause?

This isn't really about sex after all

I'm an engineer by training. A large part of my day job is troubleshooting or post-failure analysis. While I've observed a fair amount of installation and design problems in my time, I'm continually surprised at how many problems are caused by either using the equipment incorrectly or using it improperly in conjunction with other things. While there are a significant number of users who just don't understand how to use our products correctly, I've had the "Why can't I do it that way" argument many times. When in that situation, my answer is always, "That's not the way it's designed. You can do it that way if you like, but it won't work as you want it to."

As part of the counter-attack to the sexual revolution, the church has insisted on the purpose of marriage — in part. This is part of the reason we're losing the argument: we didn't tell the whole truth. Yes, marriage is a lifelong commitment, but it's much more than that. Yes, it's only between a man and a woman, but why does that matter? Yes, it's a civil ceremony with larger implications for the wider community, but it's much richer and deeper than that. It's the more, the why, and the richer and deeper parts that we overlooked, and we're now reaping the bitter harvest. For example, our lack of thought and understanding betrays us every time we hear some co-habiting celebrity denigrate marriage as "just a piece of paper." We get irritated because, in our guts, we know that's not right — but then we say nothing because we're stumped.

Some corners of the Western church, especially the more conservative ones, see (in part) the danger of our sexual libertinism and are trying to stand athwart the new zeitgeist. In a classic example of Freudian projection, the world often counter-charges that we're too hung up on sex and talk about it too much. "Live and let live," they argue. Many in the pews seem to agree, but should we? The short answer is no. Sex is the figurative canary in the coal mine. A misunderstanding of the body's design and purpose will most often fuel sexual sins first, and others, in the service of the sexual idols, will follow. That's part of what was going on in Corinth during the Apostle Paul's time, and it's what we see in our culture.

How many sophomore philosophy students have asked, "What does it all mean?" As a reformed Calvinist, I submit that the meaning of life is "to glorify God and enjoy him forever."[2] Other Christian denominations and traditions would answer similarly. If the biggest picture — human existence — has a meaning, it follows that the individual pieces also have meaning that works toward the larger meaning. How many of us in trying times have quoted, "... all things work together for good for those who love God and are the called according to his purpose"? (See Rom. 8:28). As Christians, we hold that even the bad things in life are used by God to further his purposes for his people. That infuses them with purpose — we might say meaning — that makes them bearable, even if we don't know exactly what that purpose is. Therefore, if human existence has meaning, then the pieces of human existence have meaning, and that includes our bodies.

We might respond, "Well, of course, I guess..." — but is that

---

2   *Westminster Shorter Catechism*, Answer to question 1.

how we live? I contend that it isn't. We are, counter to the Apostle Paul's command to **not** be conformed to this world, we are instead thoroughly conformed and **not** renewed by transforming our minds. (See Rom. 12:2.) This begs the question, if the gospel isn't informing us, what is?

A poor substitute for the gospel

Due to a complicated set of circumstances, I was once on a job in West Africa in lieu of a gentleman from the United Kingdom. Having little to no idea what I was doing, I had him on the phone almost the entire time, since he knew exactly what he was doing. Near the end of the job, we had completed almost all of what we set out to do, and he told me, "If you want to get something done, send an American!" Why do Americans have such a reputation? Because of slogans like, "What the mind can conceive, the will can achieve," "Believe you can and you're halfway there," and "Whether you think you can or whether you think you can't, you're right!"

While those sayings may have originated in the business world, the sentiments they express didn't. Their godfather is a philosophy called existentialism. Existentialism holds that there is neither God nor transcendent moral law and then attempts to work out a coherent philosophy from that point. One of its more famous axioms is "existence precedes essence."[3] What this means is that you and I come into the world with no meaning, and our lives and the events in them have no meaning. There's no one out there, so we have no external guidance on how to live.

However, we can't live without meaning, so we need to create one and impose it on our lives. It doesn't matter what that meaning is, so long as we create it. For example, it's just as valid and meaningful to help a little old lady across the street as it

3   John-Paul Sartre, from *Existentialism and Humanism*, translated by Carol Macomber pg. 20. Without getting too technical, the earlier Existentialists did hold that this maxim only rigorously held for people.

is to hit her on the head and steal her purse.[4] While that may offend our moral sensibilities, the Existentialists would reply that there are no "morals" in the absolute sense, since morals require someone above us to set them down.

Existentialism was implicitly rejected at the Nuremburg trials.[5] The surviving Nazis argued that they should not be judged by the "alien value system"[6] of the Allies. After all, it was just as valid for Germany to kill Jews and conquer their neighbors as it was for the Allies to fight back and liberate the concentration camps. The court rejected these arguments, and the Nazis were convicted of war crimes.

However, while no one uses the term in popular culture anymore, existentialism is strangely alive and well in the West. That's what's behind the "follow your heart"[7] ethos of our day. Your heart tells you that you're gay? Then you are. Your heart tells you that you're really a woman deep inside, no matter what your DNA and anatomy say? Then you're a woman, and you should consider taking some hormones and getting some surgery to impose your meaning on your body. There's no sense in arguing with it. After all, being a woman has nothing to do with anatomy. **Acting** like a woman is what makes you one. You can "identify" as a woman even if you have male anatomy. Besides, "The heart wants what it wants."[8]

And if the heart wants its body to be rearranged? As long as I consent, so what? If my body has no purpose or meaning, it doesn't matter what I do with it. To paraphrase Dostoyevsky, if

---

4   Francis Schaeffer, *The God Who Is There* (Intervarsity Press, Downers Grove, IL, 1998), pg. 38-39.
5   The exact differences between existentialism and nihilism (the philosophical underpinnings of Nazism) are irrelevant for the purposes of this discussion.
6   John Warwick Montgomery, *The Law Above the Law* (Minneapolis, MN, Dimension Books/Bethany Fellowship, 1975), pg. 24—25.
7   See Jer. 17:9 and Rom. 7:15-24.
8   Woody Allen, in an interview with Walter Issacson for *Time*, found at http://content.time.com/time/magazine/article/0,9171,160439,00.html, last accessed March 18, 2020.

there is no God, then all things are permissible.[9] If science can figure it out, I should be able to do it. Any reservations are merely an irrational qualm left over from a bygone, unscientific era. While the older Existentialists would acknowledge that reality limits the choices that we can make (the term that Sartre uses is "facticity"[10]), their philosophical descendants now demand that reality conform to their desires. If there's no objective truth and no objective meaning, then reality is what I make of it.

A 15th century Maori hunter or an African tribesman might retort that, "Those whom the gods would destroy, they first drive mad." Some outside the academy might brush it off under the maxim that, "One has to belong to the intelligentsia to believe things like that: no ordinary man could be such a fool."[11] To brush it off would be a huge mistake. The academy takes these ideas seriously and is pressing them with all the fervor of a religious crusade.

Sola Scriptura vs. *Nuda Scriptura* — they aren't the same

There is another problem, and it's the most difficult one to address. One of the most fundamental problems that we Protestants have is that the Bible doesn't have any verses that directly address some of the problems that we face. For example, there's no, "Thou shalt not get an abortion" or, "Thou shalt identify as the sex of thy body." That's why we often end up speechless in the face of such inanities as, "Jesus never said anything about homosexuality." We may know our verses, but we're not thinking biblically. We've been content with the pieces, and we haven't put them together as a coherent whole.[12]

9   Fyodor Dostoyevsky, *The Brothers Karamazov*, Book 11, Chapter 4.
10   Nigel Warburton, *Philosophy: The Classics*, 4th Ed. (Routledge, NY, NY 2014), pg. 235.
11   George Orwell, "Notes on Nationalism" found in *Collected Essays* (Fletcher and Son Ltd, Norwich, UK 1961), pg. 301.
12   This problem has long been noted in evangelicalism. Francis Schaeffer was

Part of the problem is that we don't understand what we teach. To the chagrin of my Catholic friends, I write this as a Protestant. The foundation of all Protestant teaching is a doctrine called *Sola Scriptura*, Latin for "Scripture alone." There are several ways to state it, but for the purposes of this book, I will use the following:

> The whole counsel of God concerning all things necessary for His own glory, man's salvation, faith and life, is either expressly set down in Scripture, or by good and necessary consequence may be deduced from Scripture...[13]

Please note that this is emphatically not what some have classified as *Nuda Scriptura* (Latin for "naked Scripture"), which is the idea that only what is explicitly stated in the scriptures is required to be believed, independent of historic Christian teaching.[14] That allows the individual to insert his private interpretation of the scriptures for what they actually teach — and, more often than not, it leads to heresy. What *Sola Scriptura* teaches is that

> The supreme judge by which all controversies of religion are to be determined, and all decrees of councils, opinions of ancient writers, doctrines of men, and private spirits, are to be examined; and in whose sentence we are to rest; can be no other but the Holy Spirit speaking in the Scripture.[15]

The scriptures are the supreme and final judge, not the only judge. Church history can be a useful guide. As a priest once told

first, and Oz Guinness has followed in his footsteps, most notably in his work *Fit Bodies, Fat Minds.*
13   *Westminster Confession of Faith*, Chapter 1, section 6.
14   https://www.thegospelcoalition.org/article/sola-scriptura-radical-ized-and-abandoned, accessed June 26, 2018.
15   *Westminster Confession of Faith*, Chapter 1, section 10.

me about heresies, "There aren't any new ones. We've seen this all before." The presentation may be novel, but the underlying ideas and desires aren't. The church is called in every age to proclaim the truths of Scripture in a language that the surrounding culture can understand, even if it must use language that isn't explicitly found in Scripture.

For example, a cornerstone doctrine of the church universal is that of the Trinity. Simply stated, we believe that the Godhead exists as three persons: the Father, the Son, and the Holy Spirit. We hold that each person is "the same in substance, equal in power and glory."[16] This is explicitly taught nowhere in the New Testament and must be inferred from several passages. Many famous heretics and their spiritual descendants have caused a lot of trouble for the church over the years by denying this doctrine. Even with all that, no orthodox Christian — Catholic, Eastern Orthodox, or Protestant — will deny the doctrine of the Trinity. Even though there is no verse that explicitly states it, it is more biblical to use non-biblical words like "Trinity" to affirm the divinity of Christ than to argue, with Arians and Jehovah's Witnesses, that since he's the Son of God, Jesus must have had a beginning like all other sons.[17]

As with the Trinity, in many discussions about bodiliness, marriage, and sexuality, thinking biblically means not looking exclusively to the Scriptures to make our case. We need to look at the facts through a scriptural lens. Before objecting too vigorously, I submit that this is exactly what the author of Proverbs does. Some of his maxims are based explicitly on the truth that God has revealed up to that time, while others are based on him looking at the world through Bible-colored glasses.

---

16   *Westminster Shorter Catechism*, Answer to question 6.
17   John Piper, "Thoughts on the Sufficiency of Scripture, What It Does and Doesn't Mean," http://www.desiringgod.org/articles/thoughts-on-the-sufficiency-of-scripture, last accessed October 26, 2017.

If we hold to *Nuda Scriptura*, then how would, for example, a Christian airline pilot get guidance for his trade? The Bible doesn't say anything about flying. Is he left to his own wits? No. "Whatever your hand finds to do, do it with your might" (Ecc. 9:10) tells him to study his craft diligently. Having flown many times, I'm grateful that pilots know what all the knobs and gauges do and mean. I would like them to not be physically impaired, either through lack of sleep (Ps. 127:2) or substance abuse (Prov. 20:1 and 23:29-35; Isa. 28:7).

While a full discussion of *Sola Scriptura*[18] is beyond the scope of this book, even the definitions I reference above, definitions that were written by strident anti-Catholics, acknowledge that the Bible does not contain all knowledge and does not **directly** answer all our questions about the world. We must think about the world and how the word of God addresses it. We need to first understand what we believe, and then understand accurately what the world says, so that we can truthfully engage them on their own ground. Paul himself does this in his Mars Hill discourse in Acts 17. He doesn't quote from the Hebrew scriptures once. However, he notes their own religious background, specifically their altar to the unknown God (v. 23), and quotes from the poet Epimenides's *Cretica*: "In him we live and move and have our being" (v. 28).

Through all that, Paul never abandons his goal of proclaiming the gospel of Christ. That's the trick for us. If we're not grounded in the truth first, encounters with the world will sweep us away with their philosophies — which is exactly what's happened with large sections of the church in the West.

The advantage of this is that it sneaks truth through what C.S. Lewis called the "watchful dragons"[19] of the world. Humans

---

18 For a fuller discussion, please see James White, *The Roman Catholic Controversy*, Chapters 2 and 3.
19   C.S. Lewis, "Sometimes Fairy Stories May Say Best What's to Be Said", found in *On Stories: And Other Essays on Literature* (Harcourt, Inc., Orlando, FL 1982), pg. 47.

are not dispassionate observers, objectively evaluating facts as they come in. Very often, we have an agenda behind believing the things that we do.[20] Sometimes, people will automatically tune us out if they think we're just quoting verses. If we think biblically instead, with the verses in the background, we'll live differently — which will be a much more powerful witness than our words.

That's the final key. As Francis Schaeffer famously asked, "How should we then live?"

20   For a powerful (and depressing) example of this, see John Piper, *A Godward Life*, (Multnomah Publishing, Sisters, OR 2006), pg. 305-306.

Chapter 2

As It Was in the Beginning

A business that I once worked for was developing a new product. It was a quantum step forward from our old product and involved a radical rethinking of the ways we had done things before. There was, however, a big problem. The marketing manager in charge of the new product insisted that we should not write any help documentation for it whatsoever. His rationale was that smartphone apps didn't have help functions because a well-designed app was so intuitive and easy to use that help functions were unnecessary. He argued that if we had to tell users how to operate our product, we had failed in making it intuitive and easy to use.

Leaving aside the wisdom of the manager's comparison of a smartphone app and a complex engineering/maintenance tool that was intended for a desktop computer (and the doubtful veracity of his assertion that smartphone apps don't have help functions), don't many of us in the church feel that way about marriage and sexuality? We look at "gay marriage," the seemingly-myriad "gender identities," three-genetic-parent children, and wonder why people can't just instinctively understand how wrong such things are.

That's the low hanging fruit. If we can't explain these, what do we do with subtler questions? What about the college sophomore who doesn't ever want to get married because his biological parents' marriage (if there even was one) failed, and who finds himself caught in the college hook-up culture? What about the 45-year-old woman who has never married, and longs for a husband? How do we handle divorced Christians who remarry? What do we teach children who've grown up in a culture where barely hidden nudity is ubiquitous and the grossest forms of pornography are an internet connection away? Why do purity pledges and rings and willpower fail? In short, when we have questions about marriage and family, where should we start?

Starting at the right place

I suggest that we start with what Jesus had to say on the matter:

> And Pharisees came up to him and tested him by asking, "Is it lawful to divorce one's wife for any cause?" He answered, "Have you not read that he who created them from the beginning made them male and female, and said, 'Therefore a man shall leave his father and his mother and hold fast to his wife, and the two shall become one flesh'? So they are no longer two but one flesh. What therefore God has joined together, let not man separate." (Mat. 19:3-6)

Before proceeding any further, these verses need a little background. In Jesus's time, there were two main schools of thought on divorce in Judaism, both referencing the divorce law in Deuteronomy 24. The first, the school of Hillel, held that a husband could divorce his wife if she displeased him, and the displeasure could be something as minor as burning a meal. Yes, Hillel was literally teaching that you could divorce your wife for burning the biscuits at supper. The school of Shammai taught that the only grounds for divorce were sexual sin, which he interpreted as being the unclean thing referenced in Deuteronomy 24:1. Both schools taught that a divorcee could remarry, subject to the restrictions given in Deuteronomy 24:2-4.

While Jesus does come down clearly on Shammai's side, he takes it one step further. Jesus doesn't even mention the Mosaic law in this part of his answer — he goes all the way back to creation itself. He doesn't start with the law; he starts with how people are made. This is where we've gone wrong. While the law is important, in this case, we should start where Jesus does, at the very beginning. We cannot hope to understand what marriage should be unless we think deeply — more deeply than we have recently — about what marriage was originally supposed to be. We will return to Jesus's words later, especially since he addresses the state of the world as it is in the next part of his answer, but to help us understand why things are so wrong, we need to understand how they should be.

Genesis 1-2 gives us two views of the creation of humanity. Genesis 1 provides a "top level" view, with the creation of man from God's perspective. Genesis 2 provides a "bottom level" view, with the creation of humanity — more specifically, woman — from man's perspective. These texts give us three divisions of "originality:" Original Solitude, Original Nakedness, and Original Communion.[1]

Original Solitude refers to the uniqueness of man in the created order. This manifests in two ways. First, he is created in

---

1   This follows the thinking of John Paul II in *Theology of the Body* 5-12.

the image and likeness of God (Gen. 1:28). Theologians use the Latin term *Imago Dei* (literally, "image of God") to refer to this. While much has been written and preached over the years about what exactly this means, we can say, at the very least, that this invests man with inherent dignity and responsibility.

After his creation, he is given the first job assignment: to tend and care for the Earth (Gen. 1:28). This is confirmed by his naming of the animals in Genesis 2. That brings us to the second manifestation of Original Solitude: authority. This is one of those subtle scriptural clues that we can miss if we don't think like an ancient Middle Easterner. To someone from that place and time, to name someone or something was to have authority over it. This means that our position at the top of the physical order is neither an accident nor a fortuitous evolutionary leap. Our position has purpose, or meaning, if you will.

One of those meanings is to image God's authority over the physical creation by caring for it. God could have set up the world like a glorified machine, requiring no outside intervention to function properly and beginning in its fullest state. Even granting his wish to delegate this task to others, God simply could have created more angels to do it. Instead, he created physical, ensouled beings. Why?

One common way to refer to man is as a "rational animal." This combines two truths; we are different from the physical order (rational), and yet we are simultaneously part of the physical order (animal). As rational animals, we are incarnate spirits and spiritualized bodies,[2] amphibians,[3] if you will. We humans, through our bodies, manifest the invisible spiritual realm to the physical world. As originally designed, we are God's delegates to care for the world. We were also to display the wisdom of God to

---

2   Christopher West, *Theology of the Body for Beginners* (Ascension Press, West Chester, PA 2009), pg. 6.
3   C.S. Lewis, *The Screwtape Letters* (New York, NY, Touchstone, 1996), pg. 40.

the angelic hosts (1 Pet. 1:12).

Before assuming that animals can't see or don't care about the spiritual realm, we should remember two things. First, given that the physical and spiritual were perfectly integrated at the completion of creation, we have no reason to believe that animals don't care about or have any connection to the spiritual. Until Immanuel Kant, no one in the West disputed that animals had souls, although there was consensus that an animal's soul did not survive the death of its body. If animals have souls, they must have some connection with the spiritual realm, although it is not on the same level as ours.

Second, we have scriptural evidence that animals at least perceive some of the spiritual realm. In Numbers 22, the sorcerer Balaam is riding his donkey to an appointment to curse Israel. He has incurred God's wrath by doing so, and an angel stands in the road to kill him. Three times, the donkey sees the angel and refuses to go forward. Balaam, not seeing the angel, repeatedly beats the donkey. After the third time, the donkey starts a conversation with Balaam, after which he sees the angel and does some swift backtracking.

I don't want to press this too far. Plants and animals do not worship God as we humans do,[4] and part of the *Imago Dei* is that we can glorify God by more than just existing. We can and should actively praise and give God glory. As rational beings, we can relate to God in a way that is above the rest of creation. We serve as a bridge of sorts between the physical world and God. One term that some theologians use to describe this bridging is "vice-regent." The vice-regent goes out in the name and with the authority of the one who sent him. Note that this is not total authority. This places limits on what we may do.

The third aspect of Original Solitude is uniqueness. Man is

---

4   This doesn't mean that they don't do it at all. See 1 Chron. 16:33 and Psalm 19.

simply unlike the rest of physical creation. One of the most pernicious results of modern evolutionary thought is the assertion that man is merely the one animal that made the evolutionary leap, and the world would be better off without him, or at least with many fewer of him. Contrary to that, another outworking of the *Imago Dei* is that nothing else in all creation, not even angels, is made in the image and likeness of God. Given this, we can say that, in the original design, man is the solution, not the problem. In addition, as an image-bearer of God, man — in his body, remember — is a walking road sign. C.S. Lewis's Screwtape notes that God's aim is to fill the world with "loathsome little replicas of himself."[5]

Before going any further, we need to consider how much giving God is doing here. First, no one and nothing deserves to be created. The bare fact of existence for both man and the rest of creation is a gift from God. Second, man and the physical creation are gifts to each other. Man's purpose is specifically to serve as God's vice-regent, stewarding creation. The creation needs man, and receives him as a gift for its betterment, even if it is not fully aware of the gift. As a gift to man, creation allows him to provide for his needs, such as food and shelter. It also provides him with fulfilling work — far more in the beginning than we have now on this side of the fall. Originally it was more immediately rewarding, since nothing was working against him or failing to respond to his care.

Another aspect of gift is that we have no record of Adam ever asking for a mate.[6] Per the Genesis 2 account, God creates man, notes that it is not good for him to be alone — and then immediately sets him to naming the animals. As an engineer by training, that strikes me as very strange at first glance. If his problem is aloneness, why not make another person immediately?

5   *The Screwtape Letters*, pg. 41.
6   Al Molher, "Homosexual Marriage as a Challenge to the Church: Biblical and Cultural Reflections," found in *Sex and the Supremacy of Christ*, ed. John Piper and Justin Taylor (Crossway Books, Wheaton, Ill, 2005), Pg. 110-111.

Why send him through what seems to be a pointless exercise?

The exercise isn't pointless. It has two very important purposes. The first is to point out to Adam that he needs fellowship with another human. God is revealing Adam to himself.[7] While naming the animals, Adam has surely noticed that there are males like him, and females, who are not quite like him. I don't think it took him very long to wonder where the female human was, and if he wondered about that, it awoke in him the understanding that, as a person, he needed other people, even though he walked with God in perfect fellowship up to that point. It likely also helped him understand his own masculinity. While bodies are more fundamental to being human than being male or female,[8] masculinity and femininity are integral to what it means to be a human. As the only man currently alive, Adam can only learn this in communion with another, female, human. As a person in communion with another person, the most intimate communion is to be naked. Again, note the emphasis on the body.

Observe that God doesn't create another man. He makes a different incarnation of a human, a female. In the divine assessment, the absence of woman, a sexually different human, is "not good," and her presence makes it "very good." Why? Because man and woman together as husband and wife also manifest the *Imago Dei*. While individual men and women are created in the image of God, that image is more fully expressed by man and woman in wedlock. Even two men or two women as deep friends do not express the *Imago Dei* as fully as a husband and wife. The differences between man and woman more fully display the attributes of God, however dimly.

That leads to Original Nakedness. Why were the man and woman "naked and not ashamed?" What was there to be

---

7   See, for example, *Gaudium et Spes* 24; "...man...cannot fully find himself except through a sincere gift of himself." This passage significantly influenced John Paul II throughout *Theology of the Body*.
8   *Theology of the Body* 8:1.

ashamed of? Nothing. Nakedness had a different meaning then than it does now. Unclouded by sin, Adam and Eve were perfectly free to "be themselves" in front of each other. They were in full control of their sexual desires and expressed them in completely appropriate ways which mutually affirmed their dignities. There was no need to hide anything, and they were fully accepting and loving of each other. Adam's song on awakening begins with "At last, this is bone of my bone and flesh of my flesh" (Gen. 2:23, NASV).

We might think of it like this: "At last! This beautiful person is like me and came from me!" When he saw Eve, Adam was bowled over by her beauty, and not just her physical beauty. Eve was so integrated in her body and soul that her "Eve-ness" shone through. Adam, as a perfectly integrated person himself, perceived all of Eve that he was capable of perceiving, and she perceived him in the same way. Did they fully understand each other? I doubt it. They probably didn't fully understand themselves, but they had enough capacity to perceive each other's beauty and desire more of it.

For further evidence of this, we look to the Transfiguration. While we don't have the full details, I think it's safe to say that Moses and Elijah were temporarily incarnated. Luke's account (Lk. 9:28-33) records that the disciples were asleep until Moses and Elijah were leaving. If they slept through the whole conversation that Jesus had with them, how did they know that it was Moses and Elijah? I submit that Moses and Elijah were so well integrated, even in their temporary bodies, that their "Moses-ness" and "Elijah-ness" shone through. [9]

While I've already alluded to it, this leads to Original Communion, and this communion finds its apex in marriage. Not only does it reveal more of the man to himself and the woman to herself[10], but marriage itself is part of the *Imago Dei*. How? God

9   I am indebted to Dr. Arnold Lumsdaine for this insight.
10   *Theology of the Body* 14:5.

himself exists as self-giving fellowship, eternally three persons in one God. These persons give themselves to each other fully, in a love that goes beyond our comprehension.[11] It therefore makes sense that, to image himself more fully, he would create beings that reflect that fellowship.

This makes marriage itself iconographic. This will be covered more deeply later, but we note that, from the beginning, road signs — icons, as the Orthodox would put it — towards the Trinity are imprinted in our very nature.

Now that God has created a human man and woman, he personally presides at their wedding. From it come the words that are used in some form at many Christian weddings: "For this cause shall a man leave his father and his mother, and cleave unto his wife, and they two shall become one flesh" (Ephesians 5:31 KJV).

This is an initial revelation of the meaning of marriage: Original Communion. How is that communion expressed? Through the body. This is what sets marriage apart from all other human relationships, as rich and beautiful as they might be. In a word, sex. Immediately after marrying them, God sends the new husband and wife out with a benediction: "Be fruitful and multiply and fill the earth and subdue it, and have dominion over the fish of the sea and over the birds of the heavens and over every living thing that moves on the earth" (Gen. 1:28). We see everything that we saw before, albeit in a different order. Nakedness is implied in multiplying, dominion is explicitly stated, and uniqueness is implied in the dominion.

However, something new has been added to the list, an expansion of nakedness, multiplication. This isn't the first

11 Johnathan Edwards goes so far as to argue that the love the Father and the Son have for each other is how the Holy Spirit proceeds from them. For further details, see "An Essay on the Trinity" in *Treatise on Grace and Other Posthumously Published Writings*, ed. Paul Helm (James Clark and Co. Ltd, Cambridge 1971), pg. 108, quoted in John Piper, *The Pleasures of God* 2nd Edition (Multinomah, Sisters OR 2000), pg. 44, footnote 24.

time that multiplication has been mentioned. It was mentioned previously in Genesis 1:22, after God creates birds and fish. The first part of the pattern is the same: "be fruitful and multiply." What's the difference between animals and humans? The *Imago Dei*. Sex, amazingly, has been swept up into the icon. This, again, shows man's link to both the creation and the Creator, since this is also how the animal kingdom multiplies, but sex has been infused with new meaning.

That new meaning is a visible expression of the unity of the Godhead. A classic statement of the nature of the Trinity is that we worship three persons in one God. The Nicene Creed explicitly states that Jesus is "of one substance with the Father," and implies that the Holy Spirit is as well, since he "with the Father and the Son together is worshiped and glorified."

To see the similarity to human life, note how Paul condemns the Corinthian church's blasé views on sex when he admonishes them with this warning:

> ...do you not know that he who is joined to a
> prostitute becomes one body with her? For, as
> it is written, "The two will become one flesh."
> (1 Cor. 6:16, quoting Gen. 2:24)

In sexual union, we have two people in one body, pointing towards three persons in one God. I grant that the analogy is incomplete, but that's part of the point. The road sign that reads "180 miles to Nashville" isn't Nashville itself, nor could it ever be.

Marriage is about us, and about more than us

As we might expect, Genesis 2 isn't the last word on marriage and sex in the Bible or even the Old Testament, but very little is said about marriage *per se*. There are marital and sexual laws in Leviticus and Deuteronomy, and several of the Proverbs speak on it, but there doesn't seem to be any of the type of teaching that we get from Paul in the New Testament. However, it's a mistake to assume that the Old Testament isn't shot through with marital imagery. It is, but the imagery points beyond itself to something even greater than the *Imago Dei*.

Paul helps us to see what that something is:

> For no one ever hated his own flesh, but nourishes and cherishes it, just as Christ does the church, because we are members of his body. "Therefore a man shall leave his father and mother and hold fast to his wife, and the two shall become one flesh." This mystery is profound, and I am saying that it refers to Christ and the church. (Eph. 5:29-32)

John Paul II calls marriage the "primordial sacrament."[12] Read through the Old Testament, especially the prophets, and over and over again, the image of God betrothing himself to Israel or marrying Israel comes up. However, the Old Testament has a reputation outside the church (and even inside it to a lesser extent) of showing the cranky and wrathful God who strikes people with destruction and death for just about anything. While that isn't true, there's one Old Testament book that especially puts the lie to that notion: the Song of Solomon.

At first blush (pun intended), it seems out of place. It's only one of two books in the entire Christian canon (Esther is the other) which doesn't mention the name of God. On a surface reading, it appears that God isn't even in view. It's an ancient Middle Eastern erotic love poem. The lovers can barely constrain their desire, as evidenced by the repeated refrain, "Do not awaken love until it desires" (Song 2:7, 3:5, and 8:4, NIV). In addition to the restrained eroticism, it seems remote from our experience.

---

12   *Theology of the Body* 19:4.

I have never told my wife that her stomach was "like a heap of wheat" (Song 7:2), and while she might indeed be dumbstruck if I did, it wouldn't be for the reason I might like. So why is it even in the Bible?

The traditional Christian interpretation was to view it strictly as a metaphor for the relationship between Christ and the church. More modern interpretations have argued that it should be taken at face value as a love song between a man and a woman.[13] Some who hold the latter view argue that the Song of Solomon is in the canon to affirm that rightly-ordered marital love is a good and wholesome thing, and that's just about as far as we can take it.

What if the correct way to read the Song of Solomon isn't just as an allegory or a literal reading, but a combination of the two? What if, as 20th century theologian Karl Barth suggested, it's an extended commentary on Genesis 2?[14] What Ephesians 5, Genesis 2, the Song of Solomon, and the prophets all point to is that our marriages, when properly ordered, experientially illumine the union between Christ and the church, and the union between Christ and the church, as explained in Scripture, illumines our own marriages in return.[15] As Christians, we must admit that we haven't lived this out as we should, and our culture needs it now more than ever. It provides a radically countercultural answer to the question, "What is marriage?" Our culture's answer is that marriage provides a legal relationship between two consenting adults that allows them to "define and express their identity."[16] If existence precedes essence, why not? Furthermore, the world argues that, "Why should we go through

---

13   These aren't the only interpretations, which add to the problem. For further details, please see *Introduction to the Old Testament*, Raymond Dillard and Tremper Longman III, (Zondervan, Grand Rapids, Michigan, 1994), pg. 258-263.
14   Karl Barth, *Church Dogmatics*, translated by O. Bussey, J.W. Edworth, and Harold Knight (T&T Clark, Edinburgh, UK, 1958), Volume 3, part 1, pg 313-315. Also see *Theology of the Body* pg. 550-551, footnotes 97 and 98.
15   *Theology of the Body* 90:1-2.
16   *Obergfell vs. Hodges*, 576 U.S. ___(2015).

As It Was in the Beginning

the formalities of getting a mere piece of paper to declare our love to the world? We love each other, and we're in a committed relationship, so that's all that matters."

This is wrong, and we Christians know it, but for too long we've been unable to explain why. I submit that the root problem is in the word "relationship." At first blush, there doesn't seem to be a problem. After all, isn't "relationship" what we're all about? We want proper "relationships" with each other, with our spouses, and how many times have we heard or used the phrase "personal relationship with Jesus Christ"?

The problem is that the modern concept of a "relationship" — with God or any human — is foreign to the Bible. It may serve a useful purpose as a legal term, but it leads us badly astray when applied to interpersonal affairs. No serious Bible translation that I know of uses the term. What does the Scripture use? Repeatedly, "union with Christ," "fellowship," or even "knowledge" (especially when describing sexual union) is used. This isn't pointless quibbling over words. "Relationships" can be entered and exited for a host of reasons. There are so many different grades of relationships within the classes of relationships — business, personal, romantic, sexual — that the list is effectively endless. The idea of "relationship" as we use it today didn't even exist before mid-20th century psychology.[17]

Union with Christ is the ultimate point of the Christian life. As we continue to work out the fruit of our union with Christ, we continue to be conformed to his image (Rom. 8:29). If union — or "communion" to use a synonym — with Christ is the point of our salvation, and if marriage is an icon of that, does it not follow that one of the ends of marriage is interpersonal communion, and not mere "relationship" as the world defines it? Marriage, while not a sacrament, isn't like any other rite or ritual outside

---

17   Fr. Stephen Freeman, "The Fiction of Relationships and the Fullness of Life," found at https://blogs.ancientfaith.com/glory2godforallthings/2017/01/20/fiction-relationships-fullness-life/, last accessed September 1, 2017.

39

the church. When a man and a woman marry, it is God himself who joins them (see Mat. 19:6; Mk. 10:9). This happens in every marriage, every time. This makes marriage more than a "piece of paper," a private action of the couple, or even a public action of the state.

Scripture's model of fraternity and a fraternity house

Arguably, the most important result of being conformed to Christ is learning to love. If husbands are to "love their wives as Christ loved the church and gave himself up for her" (Eph. 5:25), the first question we should ask is, "What is love?" Paul gives some characteristics in 1 Corinthians 13:

> Love is patient and kind; love does not envy or boast; it is not arrogant or rude. It does not insist on its own way; it is not irritable or resentful; it does not rejoice at wrongdoing, but rejoices with the truth. Love bears all things, believes all things, hopes all things, endures all things. (1 Cor. 13:4-7)

Modern fiction tends to focus on the romantic or sexual aspects of marriage, when marriage is even mentioned. Anyone who's been married for any length of time will testify that the feelings, while important, only carry one so far. While feelings are a part of love, the "bears all things" must take a large part of the load. We can sum up the phrase "bears all things" using the old word "fraternity." While in America "fraternity" often refers to a society of men living in the same house on a college campus, an older definition is "the quality or state of being brothers." Merriam-Webster lists "brotherliness" as a synonym.[18] While

18 https://www.merriam-webster.com/dictionary/fraternity, last accessed June 18, 2018.

not an exhaustive list, surely "fraternity" includes bearing, believing, hoping, and enduring all things.

While it's an erotic love poem, the Song of Solomon also has something to say on fraternity, but it's easy to overlook it with all the erotic imagery. Midway through the poem, the lover refers to the beloved as "my sister, my bride" (Song 4:9-10, 12, and 5:1-2). Strictly speaking, the second "my" is an interpolation, and the text more literally means, "my sister-bride." She replies with a wish that she and the lover had nursed together, wishing that he were her brother (Song 8:1). Although we might find it revolting at a first glance due to our scruples on incest, this is not unique to Israel. Similar uses of "sister" in a marital context appear in contemporary Egyptian and Syrian love songs.[19]

Even though it deals a lot with sex (albeit in a euphemistic manner), the Song reminds us with its use of "sister-bride" that great sex can't support a marriage by itself. As a friend once told me, "In a good marriage, sex is only about 20% of what makes it good. In a bad marriage, sex is 80% of the problem." When sex becomes everything, it means nothing. Good marriages must be built on fraternal love. Men and women share a common humanity, and especially for couples who are in Christ, they really are adopted brothers and sisters. Paul points towards this, not only in the Ephesians passage referenced above, but throughout his letters. If marriage is the closest, most intimate communion that we can enter in this world, then "my sister-bride" is an example of language bursting its bounds.[20]

While that may be a good introduction to the fraternal aspects of marriage, what about the sexual ones? Can we even speak of such an analogy without being blasphemous? If sex has been swept up into the *Imago Dei*, the answer is yes. While we must not devolve into crudity, we must also avoid its complementary

19 *Introduction to the Old Testament*, pg. 262.
20 See C.S. Lewis's essay "Transposition," found in *The Weight of Glory* (Touchstone, New York, NY, 1996).

sin, prudery.

What if the desire between the two lovers in the Song is a pointer to the desire that Christ and his church should have for each other? If God rejoices over his people with loud singing and quiets them with his love (Zeph. 3:17), is it that big of a stretch to believe that God could feel this way about his people? If "Earth's crammed with heaven / And every common bush afire with God,"[21] how much more do man and woman united point towards the blessedness and joy of God and his desire to share that joy with us?

He knows our griefs — even divorce

If the Song of Solomon is marriage done well, then the prophets show marriage done poorly. The prophets portray God as a spurned husband who's done everything he can to hold a marriage together, and the wife simply will not stay. She thinks that other men are more attractive (and well-endowed), have more money, and she just won't leave her former life as a prostitute until redeemed out of it (see Jeremiah 3, Ezekiel 16 and 23, and Hosea 1-3, respectively). The heartbreak and fury of the spurned husband leap off the page as we read again and again of what seems to be an irrevocably ruined marriage.

Jeremiah 3 and Ezekiel 23 show us the outcome of the idolatry/ spiritual adultery. God describes his divorce from Israel and Judah. God was gracious and faithful: they were unfaithful. It's clear that the "wives" only want the goodies that the "husband" can provide. In Ezekiel 16, God even accuses Israel of taking his money and hiring male prostitutes with it!

Does the divorce mean that God is finally finished with Israel? Some Christian commentators have argued that the existence of the church completely replaces the privileged status of ethnic Israel. However, Romans 11 tells us that the answer is a qualified

21   Elizabeth Barrett Browning, "Aurora Leigh", Book 7, Lines 850-851.

no.[22] The bare fact that Israel once again exists as a nation-state should make us hesitate to claim that God is finished with it.

This should point us to something. In my experience, when marriages end, it's usually over for good. Very rarely will divorced couples remarry, although some might still claim to be "good friends." Yet, God "has not cast away his people whom he foreknew" (Rom. 11:2 NKJV). Like Hosea, he continually pursues a bride who repeatedly rejects him. Lest we think that God's somehow "Crazy in Love," to use Beyoncé's phrase, he warns Israel — and us — that he does this for his glory. From beginning to end, that's why he does everything; not just the Exodus, the return from the Babylonian captivity, or even Christ's passion and resurrection. (see Deut 7:7; Ps. 102:15; Eze. 36:22-32; and John 18)

Amazingly, he links our good with his glory! What is good for us — redemption — serves to proclaim the greater glory of his name. When Paul teaches that "He who loves his wife loves himself" (Eph. 5:28b), he's not teaching something that God hasn't already done himself. He has united himself to his people so profoundly that he loves himself by loving them. Likewise, a husband and wife are so linked that what happens to either one also happens to the other, just like Christ and his church.

So, what's the bottom line?

The upshot of all this is that the human body, both male and female, has a spousal meaning. By "spousal," I mean "the power to express love: precisely that love in which the human person becomes a gift and — through this gift — fulfills the

---

22 I am not arguing that there are two ways of salvation, one for Jews and another for Gentiles, or that non-Christian Jews should not be evangelized. However, I am arguing that even though they are a "rebellious and stiff-necked people" (like we Gentiles), God, exercising his sovereign prerogative, is not finished with ethnic or even political Israel, even though many of them persist in rebellion against the true Messiah — just like many Gentiles.

very meaning of his being and existence."[23] In short, the spousal meaning is displayed when people give themselves as a gift of "total self-donation"[24] to another person for the other's flourishing, making a gift of themselves as God makes a gift of himself within the Trinity, or as Christ did to the church by his Passion and resurrection. Given what marriage meant in the Genesis 2 account, and its repeated iconographic use in the prophetic writings, it's reasonable to believe that marriage, in its original state, was an incarnated object lesson.

What does this spousal meaning include? It makes the spiritual world visible to the material world. It is to reflect the kindness, generosity, benevolence, and wisdom of God. Since God gives lavishly, we are to give lavishly to the world and to each other. It also expresses the original intended union of God and man. Note that, while marriage is a very rich and meaningful way to embody total self-gift, it is not the only way to do so. There are many situations where sexual union is inappropriate at best, and celibates are called to creatively give themselves to others. This is **not** a denial of their sexuality. Celibates are to embody that call in a manner appropriate to them as men and women.

If this sounds difficult, that's because it is. It was much easier in the garden, but due to the fall, we've irrevocably left that state behind. Things are significantly different under the regime of sin, and yet the original state of man and woman has much to teach us about why things are so wrong now. There is no area of our lives that sin does not pollute and warp, and the way things are now is the subject to which we turn next.

---

23   *Theology of the Body* 15:1.
24   *Theology of the Body for Beginners*, pg. 137.

Chapter 3

Not How Things are Supposed to Be

We are stardust,

We are golden ...

Billion-year old carbon

And we've got to get ourselves

   back to the garden

               (*Woodstock, by* Joni Mitchell,

                         as performed by

         Crosby, Stills, Nash, & Young)

Marital problems can be worse than anything. Not being in harmony with the one you love most in this world, the one you've been most intimate with, affects everything else. Everything else can go perfectly, and a fight with my wife can make it all in vain. Wealth can be intolerable with a discontented spouse (Prov. 21:9, 19), and marital harmony can make almost anything endurable. That, on a much larger scale, is what happened at the fall. We didn't just lose the garden; we lost the harmony with everything that was in the garden and beyond. That's what we want back. We want harmony with God, harmony within ourselves, harmony with other people, and harmony with the world, but we don't have it. Conflict with God, ourselves, others, and the outside world is the story of our lives.

How deep does the disharmony go? Did anything of God's good creation survive the fall, and if so, how much? The picture painted in the last chapter, of man serving as a bridge between the rest of creation and the Creator, now becomes a bleak picture of a far-reaching devastation of original sin. No one and nothing, from the most intimate details of our lives to the most far-flung reaches of humanity and culture, is unaffected.

Naked and ashamed — why?

When Adam and Eve ate the fruit from the Tree of Knowledge of Good and Evil, "the eyes of both were opened, and they knew that they were naked" (Gen. 3:7). At the maturation of the first human sin (Ja. 1:15), suddenly, of all the things that the author could have reported, he tells us that they knew that they were naked. This strikes us as weird. Surely, they knew all along that they didn't have any clothes on. A man smart enough to name every animal on Earth ought to be able to figure that much out, even if he's never seen clothing.

One thing that should be noted is that the Hebrew concept of "knowledge" is significantly different from the ancient Greek/ modern Western view. When we speak of "knowing," we refer to disembodied facts, such as 2+2=4. An ancient Jew reading this would think of experiential knowledge, that is, Adam and Eve understood the bare (pun intended) fact of their nudity all along. But after sin, their **experience** of nudity changed. The experience of nakedness changed because its meaning also changed.[1] The very first human sin immediately brought **sexual shame** with it. Before the fall, Adam and Eve were perfectly integrated in body and soul, giving themselves to each other without hesitation or reservations. Their bodies mediated their souls, which were in a state of perfect innocence.

That original innocence is now gone, replaced with original sin.[2] The human body now mediates (as much as it can in its new broken state) interior sin and shame. We now have something to be ashamed of. This new shame, in addition to being a side effect of sin, also serves a defensive function. The man and the woman now know, at a fundamental level, that instead of joyfully receiving from the other, the other wants to use him for selfish gratification. Even in our sinful state, we would rather be loved than used. We wear clothes to interfere with being used.

Another effect of sin is our tendency to use people. As then-Bishop Karol Wojtyla (later Pope John Paul II) pointed out during the "Age of Aquarius," we have two, and only two, choices in our interactions with other people. He begins by stating that a person is the sort of thing to which the only appropriate response is love.[3] We commonly assume that the opposite of love is hatred, or even indifference. Wojtyla argues that neither is true. One response to a person is to love, while the other is to use.[4]

Wojtyla is definitely on the right track. If love means to give oneself to another for his good, then to use someone else is to implicitly or even explicitly demean him as merely a means to my own ends, whatever I decide them to be. I don't care about his wants or needs, but will manipulate him to get what I want, and then cast him aside when he's outlived his usefulness to me.

---

1   *Theology of the Body* 27:3.
2   I define "original sin" using the *Westminster Shorter Catechism*, Answer to question 18: "... the guilt of Adam's first sin, the lack of original righteousness, and the corruption of his whole nature, which is commonly called original sin ..."
3   Karol Wojtyla, *Love and Responsibility,* translated by H.T. Willetts (William Collins Sons & Co, London, 1993), pg. 41.
4   *Love and Responsibility*, pg. 28.

Another problem is that when we use another person, we condemn ourselves to be used in return. We've "set the ground rules" of our interactions to revolve around a utilitarian calculus. We try to maximize our mutual happiness and minimize our mutual pain. The problem is that there's no commitment beyond the pleasure/pain calculus. If someone else comes along who can provide more pleasure or less pain (or maybe even both, as one judges it), then the parties dissolve their relations with each other.[5] Nowhere is this more poignant than the state of divorce in the West.

The question now arises: Is the body good? If we must wear clothes to interfere with someone else using us, does that mean that the body is intrinsically bad? No. However, the body now mediates lust and arouses disordered desire. This disordered desire is aroused in the same way that the law, "holy ... and good" (Rom. 7:12), arouses sin. The law doesn't cause sin, and the body doesn't cause lust. In the same way as "you shall not covet" awakens covetousness lurking within us (Rom. 7:7-8), naked bodies awaken sexual desire, which quickly mutates into lust without the Holy Spirit. Just as we can't go back to original innocence, we can't go back to original nakedness, either. Nakedness's meaning has irrevocably changed. Nudists have only half the truth; yes, bodies are good, but people use and look on them wrongly.

In Western culture, there are some women who would object that, since they don't feel ashamed, there is no true shame and that's the end of the matter (see Phil. 3:19 for Paul's assessment of that attitude). They attempt to turn any disapproval back on their critics, charging that, if someone looks at a woman wrongly, that's the viewer's problem alone.

Some criticisms of women in various states of undress have truly been cruel. For instance, using the term "slut" to describe

---

5   *Love and Responsibility,* pg. 39.

a woman, no matter how sexually promiscuous or immodest she is, demeans her and is unbecoming from anyone who claims the name of Jesus Christ. In addition, we who claim the name of Christ indeed have a duty to guard our eyes and hearts so we don't lust after a woman. We do this not primarily because she's another man's current or future wife (she may not be) or because we wouldn't want anyone to treat our female relatives that way (we don't; see Mat. 7:12), but because the woman possesses the *Imago Dei.*

However, all that doesn't make all the criticisms invalid or remove the problem of immodesty. John Calvin states it well when he warns against "lay[ing] snares for our neighbor's chastity by lascivious attire, obscene gestures, and impure conversation."[6] While I can't control entirely how my neighbor might sin, I can certainly influence it. Some of Jesus's harshest words were reserved for those who led others into sin:

> ...whoever causes one of these little ones who believe in me to sin, it would be better for him to have a great millstone fastened around his neck and to be drowned in the depth of the sea. (Mat. 18:6)

I have a confession to make. As a man, it is inconceivable to me that most women don't consider how sexually alluring their clothing might be when dressing. My wife had to correct me on that. She explained to me that a woman cannot fully appreciate her own beauty until someone else — ideally a man — affirms it.

Given that, and with deference to my wife, there's a growing stream in our culture that seeks to display a woman's sexuality without societal censure. In this book, I will use the term "hotness" to describe what they're after. Hotness is an overtly and overly sexualized desire to have physical beauty and affirmation of that

6   John Calvin, *Institutes of the Christian Religion*, translated by Henry Beveridge (Hendrickson Publishers, Peabody, Mass 2011), 2:8:44.

beauty. They may not want men running after them drooling, but they do want their sexual allure to be noticed, and, in our culture, the more of a woman's body that she exposes, the more sexual that exposure tends to be.

How should we think about nudity?

The ultimate exposure is total nudity, so what does our analysis say about post-fall nudity in general? One important point to be made is context. A nude picture, even if a close-up, in a medical textbook carries a different connotation than a nude in *Playboy*. The context in the former is to instruct and ultimately heal. The context in the latter is self-admittedly "Entertainment for Men." The medical textbook seeks to give life; the *Playboy* seeks to take pleasure without giving anything transcendent in return.[7]

How do we define nudity? Should we all, not just women, walk around in burkas, only exposing our eyes and hands, and then only because we must? This might strike some as a legal question, but I think the law in this case takes its cues from how we instinctively act, instead of the other way around. For example:

> "Nudity or state of nudity means the showing of the bare human male or female genitals or pubic area with less than a fully opaque covering, the showing of the female breast with less than a fully opaque covering of the areola, or the showing of the covered male genitals in a discernibly turgid state."[8]

What is interesting about this definition is that it demands that everything be covered which definitively identifies us as male and female. Even if the positive law didn't explicitly follow

7   See *The Screwtape Letters*, pg. 44.
8   Tennessee Code Annotated, 39-13-511 (a) (2)(A).

what we do, we instinctively cover those parts, and feel shame — societally enforced shame at that — if we don't. In addition to covering those parts of us that identify us as male and female, the Bible further teaches us that they should be covered in sexually appropriate ways. "A woman shall not wear a man's garment, nor shall a man put on a woman's cloak, for whoever does these things is an abomination to the Lord your God" (Deut. 22:5, cf. 1 Cor. 11:14).

Why does it matter? Since the body mediates sin and invites lust, we shouldn't expose it. But if we can't expose it, how are we to properly display our respective masculinity and femininity, which have been given to us by God? Through clothing.

What about art? The nude, especially the female nude, has been a rich source of artistic inspiration over the years. Even in its fallen state, the human body is still part of the apex of God's creation. However, the medium is important. A statue is one thing, while film and even photography are another. The closer we get to portraying an actual person, the more careful we must be. "Live" nudity, such as in a film or a play, is to be always avoided. Nudity in sculpture or two-dimensional art, while not "live" nudity, should be handled with great care, both to preserve the dignities of the viewer and the model, and to not encourage the viewer to objectify the model.[9]

Why? We can never go back to original nakedness. After the fall, nakedness is often linked with shame, even when sexual sin and lust aren't in view. Prisoners of war and captives were often marched off naked to humiliate them. When the Old Testament was written, this was a common practice of conquering kings in the Middle East. God himself repeatedly warns about exposing shameful nakedness (see Ex. 32:25; Isa. 47:3; Mic. 1:11; Hab. 2:16; and Rev. 16:15). With respect to art, what this means is that the closer we get to an actual naked human, the closer we

9   *Theology of the Body* 62:3-4.

get to shaming an actual person. That's body-shaming before the term was even coined.

So if we can't be publicly nude or immodest, how should we then live? While a full theology of clothing would take a book by itself, St. Paul gives us some guidelines:

> Women should adorn themselves in respectable apparel, with modesty and self-control ... with what is proper for women who profess godliness ... (1 Tim. 2:9-10)

For both sexes, this passage calls us to give serious thought to how we dress.

This is not, contrary to what some have argued, a blanket condemnation of either cosmetics or jewelry. It is a condemnation of overusing either (which has been a mark of some prostitutes even down to our present day) or of flaunting either. "If you've got it, flaunt it" is a maxim that reveals the pride and self-worship to which we are prone. Strangely enough, overemphasis on what our bodies look like can actually distract from masculinity and femininity.

As a man, bodybuilders are a good example for me. I look at those men, and they definitely don't look natural. (According to my wife, women feel the same way about swimsuit and lingerie models.) When I look at the bodybuilder, I'm really looking at how massive his muscles are. He only wears briefs to better display every inch of his body. I don't ask questions about him as a person; instead, I ask questions about his body. He has been objectified. While that's an extreme example, it's the logical end of what Paul warned against (see 1 Tim. 4:8).

Beauty is in the heart of the beheld

While we normally wear clothes to keep us from being

used, we must acknowledge that this is not true all the time. Strangely enough, sin drives us to be used because we derive pleasure out of it. Swimsuit and lingerie models do this all the time, seeking to wear ever less without being totally unclothed. Why? To display their hotness. This also happens at red carpet arrivals to prestigious awards shows. It's always the women who show some skin, while the men are impeccably dressed, either in full suits or tuxedos. They're fully covered; the women aren't. Shouldn't this strike us as inherently sexist?

There is a growing backlash against defining beauty or physical attractiveness by the Hollywood starlet. In the last few years, we've seen the rise of the "body-positive" movement. One of the aims of this movement is to press for women to take a more positive view of their bodies and to stop looking to the rail-thin, unrealistic standards for feminine beauty set by fashion and lingerie houses. This is an admirable goal, and one that Christians should support.[10] We should work to eat a healthful diet, get appropriate physical activity, and view our bodies in light of the Creator's truth, not the shifting sands of fashion, style, and cultural expectations.

The problem is that the body-positive movement attempts to do this in a manner completely divorced from the Creator. Planting its feet firmly in mid-air, it advocates for women to love and care for themselves in a healthy manner — with no external grounding for why. If there's no external grounding, then there's no such thing as beauty. Women are only left with imposing their own idea of beauty on their bodies, irrespective of the outside community or world. Without this external grounding, women are still offering themselves up for objectification. The only thing that the body-positive movement accomplishes on this front is to expand the pool of women who can be publicly objectified from surgically enhanced, skinny waifs to larger, "curvy" women.

---

10   For further information, please see http://www.thebodypositive.org/.

If hotness is the fallen version of beauty, what does true beauty itself look like? We must be careful here. C.S. Lewis's Screwtape points out that Hell subtly, but constantly, shifts its suggestions on physical beauty.[11] By any objective measure, the advent of and advances in plastic surgery surely bear him out. In addition, cultural forces also play a crucial role. As recently as 2010 in my own country, a "plus-size" model wouldn't have even been considered as a viable mainstream model.

Let's review what Peter says about this:

> Do not let your adorning be external—the braiding of hair and the putting on of gold jewelry, or the clothing you wear— but let your adorning be the hidden person of the heart with the imperishable beauty of a gentle and quiet spirit, which in God's sight is very precious. For this is how the holy women who hoped in God used to adorn themselves, by submitting to their own husbands, as Sarah obeyed Abraham, calling him lord. And you are her children, if you do good and do not fear anything that is frightening. (1 Pet. 3:3-6)

Hollywood is full of "beautiful people" who are absolute terrors to work for or even be around. Their spirits don't match their physical attractiveness. In contrast, we've all known people that, while they may not look like much by the world's standards, are truly "beautiful people." What Peter's telling us is to not focus on the externals to the exclusion of the internals. A beautiful spirit will work its way out, and so will a hateful one.

So what is beauty? John Paul II gives an important clue when he describes beauty as "the visible form of the good."[12] While he's speaking about art *per se*, doesn't that line up with

11   *The Screwtape Letters*, pg. 76-77.
12   John Paul II, *Letter to Artists*, 3.

Peter's assessment? The world may wear expensive jewelry and dresses, undergo plastic surgery, and slather on makeup, but that's cleaning the outside of the cup and plate (Mat. 23:25). This is another point where our Existentialist viewpoint has failed us. Without a belief in a transcendent beauty, all we're left with is what's in "the eye of the beholder." Unfortunately, our culture has so conflated physical attractiveness with true beauty that women can feel immense pressure to lift, tuck, and hide their imperfections.

However, it won't do to misinterpret Peter and shuffle off beauty to the merely spiritual. If our bodies mediate our souls, then what does a frumpy exterior say about what's going on inside? God has designed beauty into his world, and not just the physical world, either. Even the devil himself was once the most beautiful thing in all creation (Eze. 28:12) before his fall. Is it so unreasonable to permit humans made in the image of a beautiful God to show some external beauty?

Man and woman becomes man vs. woman

Since the fall obscures the spousal meaning of the body (that man and woman are to give of themselves on a physical and spiritual level), we should also expect the world, flesh, and devil to attack not only man and woman, but to use man and woman to attack marriage itself. Where we usually see sin manifest itself in marriage is the recapitulation of poor male leadership and female usurpation.

To a reader in Moses's day, Adam was the firstborn human. As the firstborn, he "inherits" a position of authority and leadership. However, this isn't for the benefit of the oldest son alone. In Jewish society, one of the reasons that the firstborn son inherited a double share of the estate was that he was to help care for the other brothers until they could establish houses of their own, and help find suitable husbands for his sisters, all under his father's authority if the father was still alive. When the father died, the leadership of the house devolved on him.

This responsibility (especially the spiritual responsibility) is implicitly shown in Genesis 2:17 when God tells Adam not to eat of the Tree of Knowledge of Good and Evil. Note that Eve has not been created yet. We have no record that God repeated this command to her, so where did she get her flawed knowledge of it that she tells Satan in Genesis 3:3? Given Moses's emphasis in the Pentateuch (Ex. 12:26 and 13:14; Deut. 6:20 and 11:19) on the father teaching his children the things of God, it's not farfetched to assume that Adam told her, and to further assume that Adam had moral responsibility for teaching the things of God to Eve. Paul seems to carry this over into the New Testament as well (1 Cor. 14:35).

Strangely, both God and the Devil seem to confirm a family hierarchy in Genesis 3. How?[13] When Satan attacks the first family, he goes straight to Eve. If Adam and Eve are exactly the same in every way except for anatomy, it doesn't matter which one he talks to. Eve's not stupid or gullible. However, if Satan is trying to subvert the created order, it makes perfect sense.

A common source of conflict between adults and their parents occurs when the grandparents start making plans for the grandchildren without consulting the parents first. Sometimes, this takes the form of the grandparents giving the grandchildren things that the parents have forbidden (sometimes explicitly). Ultimately, this is an attempt by the grandparents to usurp or contravene the parents' authority over their children, especially if the grandparents know that the parents will give in to their children. Satan is doing the

---

13   John Piper, "Manhood and Womanhood Before Sin," found at https://www.desiringgod.org/messages/manhood-and-womanhood-before-sin, last accessed March 3, 2019.

same thing here, twice. He's directly defying God by offering the fruit to Adam and Eve, but he adds another layer to it in bypassing Adam, who has authority over Eve. Instead of dealing directly with the vice-regent of all creation, he starts with the vice-regent's "suitable helper."

Sadly, Satan's strategy works. Adam does nothing to correct Eve's bungling of God's command. Adam doesn't interpose himself between Eve and Satan, and he's not on the other side of the garden when this happens, either. The Hebrew word translated "with her" in Genesis 3:6 could also be translated as "right there with her."[14] Adam fails in his God-given duty of moral guardianship even before he eats the fruit. He's the first passive man on record, and his bad leadership continues with his blaming Eve for giving him the fruit in the first place. When God speaks with Eve, she also tries to shift the blame downward: "The serpent deceived me, and I ate" (Gen. 3:13). Instead of ruling over creation, man was ruled by it to his ruin. The satanic inversion is complete.

This is also where the battle of the sexes begins. Instead of marriage being a mutual help, it's now a mutual competition:

> To the woman he said, "I will surely multiply your pain in childbearing; in pain you shall bring forth children. Your desire shall be contrary to your husband, but he shall rule over you." (Gen. 3:16)

Before, the woman submitted to the man's joyful care. Then, she usurped his authority to help commit the first human sin. God confirms that continual competition when he says that "your desire shall be contrary to your husband." We should further note that the word translated "desire" in v. 16 is the same "desire" found in Genesis. 4:7, where God warns Cain about sin's desire to master him.

14   Larry Crabb with Don Hudson and Al Andrews, *The Silence of Adam* (Zondervan, Grand Rapids, MI, 1995), pg. 91-92.

When God judges the first family, he calls Adam from hiding instead of Eve, reinforcing the created order of Genesis 2. When Adam emerges from hiding, God speaks with him first, then Eve, then the serpent. When he passes judgement, he goes in the opposite direction with increasing intensity: to the serpent, he promises humiliation and defeat; to the woman, pain in childbearing and marital strife; to the man, creational cursing and ultimately, his own death.

Yes, submission, but there's enough to go around

Some have argued that male headship in marriage is no different than male domination and is an artifact of the fall. Since, per the argument, this subjugates woman to an inferior status, it must be removed by Christ's redeeming work.[15] Paul argues against this in several places in his letters, grounding male headship of the family in the fact that Adam was created first (Eph. 5:23; Col. 3:18; and 1 Tim. 2:8-11).

With the advent of third-wave feminism, many critics of Christianity have focused on the submission of the wife to the husband. The world hears "submission," and thinks of a brutish, domineering man who emotionally or even physically abuses his wife. Traditionally, the church has emphasized the submission of wives to husbands. While this is biblical, we must confess to our shame that it has sinfully been used to justify a host of abuses against wives (see 2 Pet. 3:16). More modern interpretations have emphasized the mutual submission[16] (Eph. 5:21) of Christian husbands and wives in part to provide a remedy

15   For example, Gilbert Bilezikian in *Beyond Sex Roles: A Guide for the Study of Female Roles in the Bible* and Aida Spencer, *Beyond the Curse: Women Called to Ministry*, as referenced by Raymond C. Ortlund, Jr. throughout "Male-Female Equality and Male Headship" in *Recovering Biblical Manhood and Womanhood*, ed. John Piper and Wayne Grudem (Crossway Books, Wheaton, Ill, 1991).

16   See *Theology of the Body* 89:1-4.

against these abuses. That's also biblical, but it too has been used for ill ends by those who wish to de-emphasize the innate differences between men and women. Are these statements then mutually contradictory?

No. The submission looks different for men than it does for women. For the purposes of this book, let's call this "asymmetrical submission." How does this work? On the large scale, using Paul's marital analogy in Ephesians 5, the church is not in charge of Christ. He is her Lord and Master, and she is to obey him in all things. However, Christ laid aside his divine prerogative to redeem the church and present it to himself "holy and without blemish" (Eph. 5:27). Jesus, amazingly, serves the church by conforming it to himself and giving it the best and highest gift possible, himself.

How does a wife submit to her husband? By following his leadership. He's ultimately in charge of the house. This may seem unjust to our democratically trained ears, but it's not, and our selective outrage is showing. We encounter hierarchy every day. As of this writing, I work for a Fortune 500 corporation. I have six layers of management between me and the CEO. Even in my personal life, I am called to obey those in authority over me, both in the civil realm and in the church. Our civic organizations also have a hierarchy. Lest we forget, even NOW (National Organization for Women) has a president and a board of directors.

So how is a husband supposed to submit to his wife? To answer that question, we need to first answer the question of how Christians are supposed to submit to each other. A good example is, "How does an elder submit to me?" By not lording it over my faith but by working with me for my joy (see 2 Cor. 1:24). He comes down to my level. I submit to him by obeying his commands, but I obey his commands for my benefit when we both are living per God's direction. This is also asymmetrical submission.

What if an elder or pastor tells me that, for example, I must give him sexual favors? The scandal engulfing the Southern Baptist Convention and the Catholic Church's sexual problems in its priesthood both display that this is not idle speculation. With respect to obedience, the only unqualified command in scripture regarding obedience is to obey God. We obey him over husbands, government, and even church authority itself (Acts 5:29).

Asymmetric submission — without both parts, neither one works

To see how asymmetrical submission works on a smaller scale, let's separate the submissions and see what happens. If we have the mutual submission without the male headship, we end up in a situation that denies the creational order. Men end up failing to lead more miserably than we do already. This rapidly works its way into the church. Egalitarians argue that if women can co-lead their own homes, then who rationally is to say that they are incapable of leading the church, or vice versa?

The argument isn't without merit. There are biblical examples of women leaders in Israel. The first example is Deborah, co-judge of Israel with Barak (Judges 4). When she tells him that the Lord has sent him against Sisera, he refuses to go into battle unless Deborah — a woman — goes with him. Any reader of the time would immediately brand Barak a coward for hiding behind a woman's skirts, even if she was a prophet.

It's easy to spiritualize this by arguing that Barak wanted God's representative to go with him, but that's more eisegesis than we would like to admit. When Judges was written, if God called a man to battle, he was expected to go, and the battlefield was especially not a place for women, who were considered incapable of standard hand-to-hand combat. That's why Sisera's death was considered so shameful (Jud. 5:24-31), because a mighty warrior was not supposed to be killed by a lowly woman.

The second example is Huldah, the prophetess in 2 Kings 22. When King Josiah orders repairs made on the temple, the Book of the Law is discovered. Hilkiah, the high priest, orders the book sent to Josiah, who immediately sends a delegation to Huldah on hearing the curses for covenant disobedience. Why wasn't Hilkiah instructing the king in the law? If he did nothing else, a high priest was at least expected to know the law. Why did the king have to eventually go to someone else for divine guidance?

The common link in these two stories is a failure of male leadership. The men were falling to lead, so God called a woman to serve him. Does God call women into leadership today? Yes — but almost always where there's a failure of the men.

We have an implicit assumption that hierarchy implies inequality. It does nothing of the kind. We are neither robots nor clones, and we are not perfectly equal in every way. However, God does intend for us to be equal in honor and dignity. Paul once again turns to the human body to illustrate his point:

> ...On the contrary, the parts of the body that seem to be weaker are indispensable, and on those parts of the body that we think less honorable we bestow the greater honor, and our unpresentable parts are treated with greater modesty, which our more presentable parts do not require. But God has so composed the body, giving greater honor to the part that lacked it, that there may be no division in the body, but that the members may have the same care for one another. (1 Cor. 12:22-25)

"Unpresentable parts" refers at least to the areas that we would define as making us nude or indecent, but there are other ways that body parts can be unpresentable. Scarring, disfigurement, injury, or the inevitable decline of age make once presentable parts embarrassing for others to look at. However, Paul notes that God has designed the human body in such a way that honor is shared, even among the parts that don't have it. (As we see in Genesis 3, so is shame.)

When we extend this to the body of Christ, the first thing that we should say is that, if submission is practiced in such a way that dishonors people, then it's not submission, but subjugation. This doesn't just apply to women. Elders can also subjugate their churches by lording it over their faith (2 Cor. 1:24). While the church may be the *militia Christi* (army of Christ), that doesn't mean that church leaders are marine drill sergeants, like Sgt. Hartman in *Full Metal Jacket*.

The second part of our analysis is the submission of the woman to the man without the corresponding asymmetric submission of the man to the woman. This reduces the woman to little more than a glorified slave. Sadly, some strains of Protestant teaching do just this.

For example, take this unfortunate commentary on 1 Corinthians 7:

> As husband and wife, we belong entirely and unreservedly to each other — my body is his possession, and his body mine. We are to give ourselves without qualification and not withhold the pleasure of sex. The only exception to this rule is for the activity of prayer and then only by mutual agreement and for a limited time. We must heed this admonition and offer no excuses. As I once heard a man say, "I've heard many

excuses for not having sex — not in the mood, headache, too tired, don't have time. Prayer and fasting has never been one of them." When we choose to obey God and give our bodies to our husbands — even if we don't feel like it — God will reward us with pleasure.[17]

As a man, that appeals to my libido, but when my wife read the above quote, she replied, "How petty! A lot of times, a woman will say she has a headache because she feels like her husband is using her." On further reflection, she wanted me to add this statement: "That's just gross. It's too formulaic."

She's right. This reduces a woman to little more than a living sex toy. She's to be always willing and available (except for prayer and fasting, of course). Her reward? Physical pleasure. Not the joy of union with her husband, or the blessing of children, just a good time. How is this different from the ubiquitous pornography that pervades our age? Is she just supposed to, as the apocryphal quote has it, "Lie back and think of England?"

We dare distill Paul's teaching down to mere dutiful sex? "Dutiful sex" is just as sexy as reading legal codes, and for most of the same reasons. To our shame, even the world knows this. Winston's first wife in George Orwell's *1984* is sexually frigid, and only acquiesces to his advances out of a sense of marital duty. Winston can't stand it, and it is a factor in the failure of their marriage.

If a couple are encountering protracted sexual difficulties, they should be encouraged to seek medical attention or pastoral counseling as necessary. However, if a husband insists on "his rights," another problem exists. How did Paul handle the question of rights? By giving them up for the flourishing of his churches (see 1 Corinthians 9). If we're treating our wives as

---

17   Carolyn Mahaney, "Sex, Romance, and the Glory of God: What Every Christian Wife Needs to Know," found in *Sex and the Supremacy of Christ*, pg. 206.

we'd treat our own bodies (Eph. 5:28-29), this won't be a problem. If we're treating wives as sexual playthings, we should expect marital problems. People know when they're being used, and they naturally rebel against it.

This doesn't just apply to the sexual, either. Taken to its logical end — divorced from mutual submission, remember — this gives the husband practical carte blanche authority over the wife. Does she think he's about to make a bad business decision? "Don't say anything and just pray about it." Is she concerned about how he disciplines the children? "Be submissive and God will change his heart." Again, the wife becomes little more than a slave.

It starts with the body, but it doesn't end there

With the advent of human sin, this sad state of affairs is the new normal, and the new normal can't stay in Eden. So after pronouncing judgement, God sends Adam and Eve out of the garden. Mercifully, he doesn't destroy them, and he gives them another mercy as well: "...the LORD God made for Adam and for his wife garments of skins and clothed them" (Gen. 3:21). Where did the skins come from? The same place that they come from today: a dead animal. Physical death has now entered the world, right on the heels of spiritual death (Rom. 5:12-14).

Now, not only is there a break between humans, there's a break between man and nature. Instead of man caring for nature and nature serving mankind, man now seeks to take advantage of nature, and nature so longer responds to man as it did. God confirms this:

> ... cursed is the ground because of you. In
> pain you shall eat of it all the days of your life.
> Thorns and thistles it shall bring forth for you ...
> By the sweat of your face you shall eat bread, till

> you return to the ground…for you are dust, and
> to dust you shall return. (Gen. 3:17-19)

Man can undoubtedly cause great levels of environmental degradation. However, it appears that, in some way that we do not completely understand, even if man were doing his best to tend the ground, it still would not produce up to its pre-fall potential. It's not just mankind that is fallen. The entire world fell with us. Why else would the Earth be cursed? If man is to serve as a "bridge" of sorts between the spiritual and the physical world, then it follows that, with the spiritual death of man, the world is, in a certain sense, cut off from God. So now that we live in a fallen world, is it still good in any sense, and what is our role in it? The world is broken, but, yes, it is still good (1 Tim. 4:4).

Then what is the role of a Christian in a cursed creation? There is a proper Christian environmentalism. Many Christians have been wary of the environmentalist movement for two reasons. First, there's a strong strain of Earth-worship going through it. Second, there's an equally strong strain of misanthropy in it as well. Like the nudists, the Earth-worshippers have half of the truth. The Earth is ours to steward, not to plunder — or to worship. This means that it is still true that more people are the solution, not the problem. With respect to the question of over-population, we can be confident that God has correctly sized the Earth for the population that he sees fit to put on it. He ultimately opens and closes the womb. While that doesn't change our responsibility to use the earth wisely and to wisely order our sexual lives, it does take the pressure off us. The Earth isn't resting on a knife's edge, waiting for us to blow it over.

While the meaning of nakedness may have changed, the creational mandate hasn't. Now that sin has entered the world, it's even more important that we use the natural world wisely to help alleviate human suffering, encourage human flourishing, and honor God by doing so.

My wife pointed out something very instructive. When the term "nature" is used today, it's almost exclusively used in a personal sense; "Mother Nature," for example. More often, instead of using "nature" to refer to the created world, we now speak of "the environment." Why the change? I suspect that "environment" reflects the schizophrenia of our culture. One side of our collective unconscious worships the Earth, while the other sees it as merely a particularly resource-rich mud ball to do with as we please. The Earth-worshippers regard the Earth as holy and are willing to sacrifice people to it. The followers of scientism regard nothing as holy and will sacrifice people in the name of "progress," like Weston in C.S. Lewis's *Out of the Silent Planet*.

Neither is what the Bible teaches. What it teaches is that the earth is ours to use as a gift, but it is also ours to steward as a task. Often, we do it badly. The stereotypical image of human misuse of the Earth is that of a barren, blasted landscape stripped of everything valuable and left in ruins or used as a toxic waste dump. However, we can also conserve the wrong things. As American philosopher Wendell Berry points out, most U.S. National Parks consist of rock or ice, which mostly can't be used anyway.[18]

We must beware of the brutal utilitarian logic of modern environmentalism. Activist Paul Erlich started the latest round with his erroneous predictions that millions of people would starve to death during the late 1960s into the 1970s, all the while insisting that population growth would outstrip food production capability. Even given the spectacular failure of his predictions, a sizeable segment of environmentalists persists in maintaining that we need radical population control measures, or we'll use up all the available resources.

18   Dave Forman, quoted by Wendell Berry in "Conservation is Good Work," found in *Sex, Economy, Freedom, and Community* (Pantheon, NY, NY, 1992), pg. 27. His point is a bit overstated. The Great Smoky Mountains National Park, near my home, would be a bonanza for loggers and miners.

Such teaching is despairing and shows not only a lack of trust in God, but a failure of imagination. Examples of mankind increasing resource yields or finding better substitutes are so numerous that Julian Simon made a career of debating such doomsayers. Mankind can be quite creative when he must be, especially if his mind is given a nudge from the Holy Spirit. He can inspire in more ways than just Scripture. Such inspiration is one of the many ways that God provides our daily bread.

The population control movement never seems to take human ingenuity or inspiration into account. They always seem to implicitly assume that all we have right now is all we'll ever have, and we must hoard it, like Ebenezer Scrooge greedily clutching his shillings. When I was younger, environmentalists called themselves "conservationists." "Conservation," I hold, is the wrong approach. To conserve something means that we set a boundary around it, declare it off-limits, and forbid ourselves to ever use it. Of course, this doesn't happen in practice. In the Great Smoky Mountains, a lot of government and volunteer work goes into maintaining hiking trails, campgrounds, and lodges. The state and federal wildlife services are attempting to reintroduce species not seen here for quite some time and preserve those that are endangered. Though ensuring that the Smokies aren't developed for commercial use, they are actively tended, so as many people as possible can enjoy them in close to their natural state. This isn't "conservation;" it's stewardship, and stewardship brings us back to the creational mandate. It's almost as if we can't help ourselves.

If the creational mandate hasn't changed, neither has the command to "be fruitful and multiply." Even in their fallen state, Adam and Eve still receive common grace when they conceive children. They give themselves to each other, and it results in a new person. Once again, as they enter their new roles as parents, each is revealed to himself in a new way.

Before, they were revealed as bodies in a world of bodies. Since being a body is fundamental to being human, this makes sense. Now, God further reveals them to themselves and each other via masculinity and femininity. Adam learns what it's like to be a father, and Eve learns what it's like to be a mother. Each learns in communion with the other to be parents.

This, too, points back to God, especially with respect to fatherhood. After all, human fatherhood is derived from God (Eph. 3:15), and God is often described as a father and husband (Jer. 31:32; Ezekiel 16; Mat. 6:9; 1 Thess. 3:13; Ja. 1:27; and 2 John 3), although he also demonstrates "motherly" qualities as well (Isa. 66:12-13; and Hos. 11:1-4).

They also experience another meaning of the body, the ability to give life. While this does include procreation, that's just a sub-set of what the life-giving meaning encompasses. In a certain sense, the creational mandate and the fecundity mandate both arise from the same fundamental principle. If God is the "giver of life," it makes sense that life giving is itself part of the *Imago Dei*.

Rather than giving life, we bring death all too often. The next human sin recorded after the fall was Cain's fratricide in Genesis 4. Human existence, while it has great joys, is marred all too often by sin and death. While physical death awaits us all, there are a thousand little deaths along the way. Friendships die, parental and filial affections die, even marriages die. If Jesus "came that they might have life and have it abundantly" (Jn. 10:10), what does that mean for these little deaths? We appear to be bent on committing suicide. How does he save us from ourselves?

Chapter 4

Managing the Fallenness

Proving that God has a sense of humor, I have found myself in the role of a teacher several times over the years. First, I had to give a day-long seminar to customers after installing one of our products onsite. I then changed jobs and found myself giving week-long courses to our customers and salesmen on our products. After being reassigned, I then made three- to five-minute videos for our products that addressed common points of confusion customers had when using them.

One thing that I quickly discovered was that some students only came to class because someone made them. They merely wanted to listen to the lectures, do the labs, get their attendance certificate, and go home. Others were truly interested not only in what they could do with our product, but also in why it operated as it did. These students were often the most successful. They understood the why so they could understand the how and what.

The converse is also true. Students with an "I don't care why, just tell me what I have to do" attitude set themselves up for trouble later. Eventually, the instructions for the standard operation fail, and users must think fast. When that time comes, knowing the "why" helps overcome the problems that life and industry invariably present.

That's true in all of life. While the rules of everyday life are necessary and get us through 99% of what we deal with, there's always that outlier that forces us to think and act differently. If we fail to understand that the "what" isn't the end, but an expression of that underlying "why," then we get stuck.

So we come back to Jesus's conversation with the Pharisees, which we discussed in chapter 2. He went past the law to discuss how people are made and what marriage is ultimately for. However, the Pharisees were still hung up on the law. The discussion continues:

> They said to him, "Why then did Moses command one to give a certificate of divorce and to send her away?" He said to them, "Because of your hardness of heart Moses allowed you to divorce your wives, but from the beginning it was not so. And I say to you: whoever divorces his wife, except for sexual immorality, and marries another, commits adultery. (Mat. 19:7-9)

The thrust of their question seems to be a mocking one: "Okay, Mr. Smarty-Pants, if marriage is indissoluble, then why does divorce even exist? After all, Moses commanded us to divorce our wives." Sadly, the legal experts read their own law incorrectly (Jn. 5:39). Jesus then reveals the sexual wickedness of their own hearts by pointing out their intransigence. "Because your hearts were hard." Not the "them" of Moses's day; the "your" of the people right in front of him. This is a tough pill for us to swallow, because the same logic applies. It's not just 1st century Jews who have a problem loving and being faithful to their spouses, it's us.

There are two usual reactions to this text. What do we often implicitly or even explicitly hear on these matters when speaking with the world, and increasingly, among ourselves? "The Bible is just not relevant. Yes, the parts about loving your neighbor are nice, and we should be kind to each other, but all that marital and sexual teaching from a bygone era was obsolete in the Enlightenment, and even more so now." This overlooks the sad fact that we are the same old people with the same old wicked desires, sinning the same old sins. The only difference is that we have fancier toys to do it with. The Jews of Jesus's time had become accustomed to divorce. The Romans were even worse. Like the Romans, we barely give it a second glance anymore, other than to say, "That's too bad," if we even do that.

The other reaction is to make the mistake the Pharisees did, and quote the scriptures without understanding why the text says what it does. This is especially problematic with the Mosaic law for two reasons. First, to use one example, the law allowed multiple wives, which is condemned in Christianity. Amazingly, God compromises with sin in the law. Why on earth would he do this? Because "the Spirit had not yet been given" (Jn. 7:39). Once we see this, some things in the Old Testament start making sense, such as the statement that David was a man after God's own heart (1 Sam. 13:14). In the Christian era, this would be unthinkable. A wife-stealing, murdering, Machiavellian who treated his wives and concubines like chattel is a man after God's own heart? (See 2 Sam. 3:13-16, 11:1-27 and 20:3.)

What was the compromise? Lust would be overlooked, sexual deviancy would not.[1] Multiple wives were allowed (but see Ex. 21:10), but incest is condemned in its various forms (Lev. 18:1-15), homosexual and bestial sex are capital crimes (Lev. 20:13 and 15-16), as was rape in certain situations (Deut. 22:25-27). Granted, some of this strikes us as repugnant today, but I submit that we only see it as such because of the coming of Christ, the

1   *Theology of the Body* 36:2.

gift of the Holy Spirit, the writing of the New Testament, and the rise of the church.

Second, in addition to the compromises with the flesh, we must look past the law because the law was weakened by sinful flesh (Rom. 8:3). It tells us not to commit adultery and, immediately, we want to commit adultery. It's not just sex. The whole law affects us this way. That's why purity rings, pledges, and sheer willpower fail. Even when we want to do good things, we end up not doing them, and do the things that we know that we shouldn't (Rom. 7:14-25). Sex out of wedlock is bad. Growing up, most Christians that I knew would admit this — and then a few of them turned up pregnant and unmarried.

With this weakness in mind, Jesus pointedly observes that Moses **allowed** divorce, instead of commanding it. In so doing, he strips the fake religious veneer off their sin. How many husbands justified turning their wives out on the assertion that, "I'm only doing what Moses commanded"? Jesus will have none of that. He repudiates a one-sided interpretation of marriage that has the woman as little better than a slave to the man.

Sadly, the Edenic curse finds its fulfillment here. Not only have husbands domineered over their wives, and not only have wives' desires been against their husbands to usurp their God-given authority, but the final outcome of marital strife has been the death of marriages. As we saw with the Hillel/Shammai divorce controversy, some divorces were nothing short of abusive, while some, due to adultery, were heart-rending. Unfortunately, that pattern still holds true today.

The disciples then react:

> The disciples said to him, "If such is the case of a man with his wife, it is better not to marry." But he said to them, "Not everyone can receive this saying, but only those to whom it is given.

> For there are eunuchs who have been so from birth, and there are eunuchs who have been made eunuchs by men, and there are eunuchs who have made themselves eunuchs for the sake of the kingdom of heaven. Let the one who is able to receive this receive it." (Mat. 19:10-12)

The disciples' logic is clear: if marriage is so fraught with peril, and if you must stay in once you're in, then to be truly holy, Christians should be celibate. Even worse, what if I make a mistake by marrying the wrong person? If rectifying that mistake causes us to sin further, then the safest course of action is to not marry at all. On a surface reading, Jesus, like Paul in 1 Corinthians 7, seems to argue that celibacy is a superior spiritual state. Is that the case?

Marriage is an option, but it's not the only option — or the best one sometimes

Not necessarily. Jesus, like Paul, is teaching that some Christians, for several reasons, are called to celibacy. At this point, we Protestants must admit that our branch of the church has done a lousy job dealing with celibacy. From the excesses of pre-Reformation Catholicism's elevation of celibacy over marriage,[2] we went to the other end of glorifying marriage at the expense of celibacy. Even today, we treat celibates as though there's something wrong with them. Our singles groups are *de facto* marriage pools. When that one comes along who just can't pair off, he ends up moving out of the group because everyone else ends up focusing on marriage.

That's a tragedy. Celibates are a vital part of the body of Christ, and those of us who are married need them more than

2   For example, Catholic canon law still allows for the dissolution of a non-consummated marriage if one of the spouses enters certain religious orders. (Council of Trent, Session 24, cannon 6). See http://www.newadvent.org/cathen/05054c.htm, last accessed June 7, 2017.

we realize. Why? Celibacy serves as a complementary function to marriage. While marriage points toward the future collective reality, celibacy points toward the future individual reality. Jesus points out that, "In the resurection they neither marry nor are given in marriage, but are like angels in heaven" (Mat. 22:30). Sad though it is to say, every marriage in this age is temporary. Even the best of them are inevitably broken by death.

However, for those who can choose celibacy by not marrying, it must not be chosen for celibacy's sake. Strange though it may sound, (with apologies to C.S. Lewis) God likes sex. After all, he invented it.[3] Celibacy must be chosen for the Kingdom of God. A single can either discern that he is not called to marriage, or recognize that, to obey Christ, he must remain celibate until he marries. In either case, celibates, merely by their celibacy, also serve as a prophetic condemnation of our age's obsession with sex.

Suggest in the West that people should not have sex for non-medical reasons and people will look at you like you've declared yourself a poached egg. This isn't a new phenomenon, either. Paul himself had to deal with this in Corinth (see 1 Cor. 6:12-20). Sex is not merely a biological process like eating or sleeping. Celibates paradoxically demonstrate this by not having sex to obey Christ. There's no corresponding command to not eat or drink. Even when fasting, Christians are only to do it for a limited time. Celibacy could be indefinite. That's not to say that married couples are disobeying Christ through their sexual activity, although they might be. I am saying that celibates fulfill a unique — and, on multiple levels, difficult— role in human society.

Some celibates have chosen it, some haven't. For the ones who haven't, celibacy can be a long, lonely, and painful road. Some have tried it who didn't have the gift. Remember, he **who is able** to receive it, let him receive it (See Mat. 19:12.)

---

3   Paraphrased from C.S. Lewis, *Mere Christianity* (Touchstone, NY, NY, 1996), pg. 65, on the goodness of matter.

Lest we think the challenges of celibacy unique to our era, we need to remember that this was even more shocking to its first audience than it is to us. In the Israel of Jesus's day, barrenness was considered a curse from God (see 1 Samuel 1 and Lk. 1:25). In an agrarian society, two things are vital for life: land and children to help work that land. In the absence of modern farming technology, the way to compensate is to have many farmhands, even if you must beget them yourself. From a practical viewpoint, this also explains why few people are called to celibacy. If people stop having babies, humanity won't be around for much longer.

For 1st century Jews, there was also the promise of the coming Messiah. He had been long promised to be Abraham's offspring (Gal. 3:16), and every Jewish girl knew that she might be the one to birth him. When Jesus not only doesn't condemn celibacy but praises it as a gift to further the Kingdom of God, his hearers must have suspected him of being either mad or possessed.

For those who don't have the gift, this is a powerful word (combined with Paul's instructions in 1 Corinthians 7) prodding us to get married. Women are not just playthings. Men, if you're going to court a woman, figure out if you can be married to her. If not, do everyone a favor and break it off. Then, discern if you're supposed to be celibate. If not, find a wife.

What about people who've had sinful sex? The good news is that God forgives those sins too. If you haven't obeyed the Scriptures, start now. Celibacy doesn't necessarily mean that you've never had sex; it means that you're dedicating your sex life to God by obeying his commands. The world tells us that we show love by having sex; celibates show their love to God by not having sex (see Jn. 14:15). Several well-known Christians had sordid sex lives before they came to Christ. Augustine fathered a child out of wedlock and lived with a concubine for years before repenting. Dorothy Day had an abortion.

An important lesson to be drawn from the monastic tradition is that celibacy is not to be attempted in isolation. The sheep are much easier for the wolves to catch when away from the herd. Remember that being incarnate is more fundamental to being human than being male or female. That means that our need for interpersonal fellowship is more fundamental than, and can be met outside of, marriage. Again, Protestantism has done a lousy job of this. We rejected monasticism and threw the celibate baby out with the monastic bathwater.[4]

So, what do we do? I think that the institution of **same-sex** singles groups would be a good place to start. Such groups should be segregated to prevent them from becoming marriage pair-off groups. These are not just social groups either. They also need to be out in the community serving in the name of Christ. The church must be courageously wise here. We should take the lead in re-discovering the art of same-sex friendship in a culture that attempts to sexualize every profound interaction between two people.

How does divorce factor into all this?

Before we move forward, we need to go back to the end of verse 9 in Matthew 19:

> ...whoever divorces his wife, except for sexual immorality, and marries another, commits adultery.

This passage is one of the classic divisions between Protestants and Catholics. Historic Protestantism taught that, if a divorce was biblically valid, a subsequent marriage was also valid. Catholicism continues to officially hold that a valid Christian

---

4   While Lutheran and Episcopal monasteries exist, those are the only two branches of Protestantism that I am aware of where they do, and their numbers pale in comparison with the Roman church.

marriage, once consummated, can only be broken by death.[5] Therefore, divorcees were required to remain celibate until either their deaths or the deaths of their ex-spouses. We must admit that, if not for this one passage, historic Protestant and Catholic teachings on divorce would have been identical, albeit for different reasons.

Is divorce a bad thing? Absolutely. God hates it (Mal. 2:16). However, we also need to acknowledge what Jesus says. Not all divorce is wrong. In this passage, he explicitly states that divorce is permissible for adultery. While a single instance of adultery is a horrible and damaging thing, reconciliation should be pursued first before proceeding to divorce. Unfortunately, if an affair is ongoing or one party repeatedly breaks his vows, reconciliation simply may not be possible. In such cases, divorce merely reflects the "fact situation," to use a legal term.

There's another passage in 1 Corinthians that we should note in conjunction with Jesus's teaching:

> But if the unbelieving partner separates, let
> it be so. In such cases the brother or sister is not
> enslaved. God has called you to peace. (1 Cor. 7:15)

Paul writes with an eye towards mixed marriages in Corinth. As with any new church, the Corinthian church was almost exclusively made up of converts. There would inevitably be situations where one spouse converted and the other didn't (1 Pet. 3:1-7 and 1 Cor. 7:16). If the converted spouse was serious about following Christ, that would also inevitably bring conflict to the marriage, because "whoever is not with me is against me" (Mat. 12:30). While the conflict might be manageable, there would be situations where one spouse wanted nothing to do with Christ or his people — including the converted spouse. Rather than put up with it, he decides to divorce her against her will.

5   The exact definition of what constitutes a valid Christian marriage in Catholicism is beyond the scope of this section.

This is also one reason that Christians should not marry known non-believers (2 Cor. 6:14).

What if both parties are professing Christians? The command of Scripture is clear: reconcile (1 Cor. 7:11). If one of the parties refuses to do so, he has not merely disobeyed the church; he has disobeyed God. He has hardened his heart against the Holy Spirit, and then a more fundamental problem exists. In such a case, it is quite possible — if not likely — that the deserting spouse is not a Christian. This dilemma is even more pointed if there's adultery going on, and one or both parties refuse to get serious in fighting sin (Mk. 9:43-47).

If there is domestic violence or non-physical abuse, then the church should take the lead in shielding the victims. Depending on the situation, it may be necessary to involve the authorities and deal with the offense on parallel tracks, both civilly/criminally and in the church. We should shun the notion that such things are properly handled in the church alone and the world just needs to mind its own business. If a husband will not repent of abusing his wife, a stay in prison may be the God-ordained tool for helping him do so. It wouldn't be the first time someone says, "Bless you, prison, for having been in my life."[6]

So, a man is divorced. What next? If the body has a marital meaning to it, what impact does a divorce have? Before moving forward, we must acknowledge that God himself is a divorcee. Ezekiel 23 gives some of the most graphic descriptions in all the Bible of what Israel's apostasy did to God, and how he reacted.

If a divorcee has remarried, we should not encourage a second divorce and a return to the first spouse. One marriage has already been broken, and we shouldn't compound the problem by breaking another. Divorce should be a method of last resort when all other efforts toward reconciliation have failed or are

---

6   Alexander Solzhenitsyn, *The Gulag Archipelago*: 1918-1956, translated by Thomas P. Whitney (Harper & Row Publishers, NY, NY, 1974) Vol. 2, pg. 617.

obviously futile. In such cases, it merely becomes a public declaration of the private reality.

Marriage, even after divorce, sets up a permanent connection between the spouses. While he's strictly speaking about mere sexual activity, C.S. Lewis's observation that sex sets up a relation that either must be eternally enjoyed or eternally endured[7] certainly applies in this situation, especially if children are involved. That relationship isn't obliterated even by a subsequent remarriage. The only thing that definitively breaks it is death, and even then, in my experience, the longer the couple were married, the deeper the survivor's connection to the spouse, even after death.

Divorce is not the unforgivable sin. Depending on the circumstances, it may not even be a sin for the offended spouse. While I have known people who threw parties when their divorces were finalized — and such people should repent — most describe it as the most emotionally wrenching thing that they have ever gone through. I begrudgingly admit that, while historic Protestantism is wrong, it's at least trying to be biblical. Modern Protestantism has abandoned biblical teaching in this area to avail itself of serial monogamy.

Can remarried people ever have sex again?

If re-marriage is sinful, is Jesus teaching that remarried Christians are in a state of perpetual sin? Catholics teach just that, unless the couple lives celibately.[8] Jesus seems to believe otherwise.[9] A critical clue is found in John 4, where Jesus has a conversation with a Samaritan woman who hasn't been a model of marital fidelity, to put it mildly. After a brief discussion, Jesus commands her:

---

7   *The Screwtape Letters*, pg. 71.
8   *Catechism of the Catholic Church*, paragraphs 1649-1650.
9   My logic in this section follows that of John Piper, http://www.desiringgod. org/articles/divorce-remarriage-a-position-paper, last accessed March 7, 2017.

> "Go, call your husband, and come here." The
> woman answered him, "I have no husband."
> Jesus said to her, "You are right in saying 'I have
> no husband'; for you have had five husbands,
> and the one you now have is not your husband.
> What you have said is true." (Jn 4:16b-18)

Notice that Jesus refers to the first five men as husbands. He doesn't say, "You lived with five men," or "You tried to have a husband," but that husbands were had. That implies that, while illicit, such marriages were valid. Given that, I hold that remarried Christian divorcees should be barred from church leadership and the sacrament until they acknowledge and confess the sin of remarriage.[10]

What then should the church do about divorcees who have not remarried? We should welcome and encourage them as celibates. If reconciliation is possible, then we should also encourage and work towards it. The process will certainly be unpleasant, but to just throw up our hands, assume a marriage is unsalvageable, and blithely let divorcees continue towards serial monogamy is to "quench the Spirit" (1 Thess. 5:19).

An objection can be raised that this doesn't show the mercy of Christ. Some were divorced against their will and worked tirelessly to keep the marriage together. Under my logic, if a divorced spouse remarries, then the other one is left to singleness at least until the ex-spouse dies. However, Jesus doesn't make any qualifiers about blame. He states that remarriage is adultery.[11] He has given divorcees a difficult calling, and we need to have the courage to face up to that. If we can't admit that with divorcees, even under the teachings of historic Protestantism,

---

10   I understand this this is a controversial position, to say the least. However, if remarriage is a sin, then it should be treated as any other sin.

11   Please see Piper's position paper referenced in footnote 9 of this chapter for a more extensive defense of why adultery by a guilty spouse does not justify a remarriage of the innocent one, specifically his analysis of the use of "μοιχεία" (moicheia) vs. "πορνεία" (porneia) in Mat. 19.

how do we face up to it when homosexuals want to marry, to give one example? If we don't take marriage seriously, why should the world? The fact that so many marriages in the church fail is not only an indictment on the couples themselves, but on a church that lets them fail without so much as a whimper, only offering milquetoast excuses like, "Sometimes, things just don't work out."

Earlier, I stated that celibacy should only be chosen for the Kingdom of God. A divorcee who's been abandoned would probably object that he hasn't chosen celibacy, and how is he supposed to live the rest of his life without companionship? Again, we need to remember that, "If you love me, you will keep my commandments" (Jn. 14:15). Love sometimes forces difficult choices on us. In this case, obeying Jesus's commands to not commit adultery **is** choosing celibacy for the kingdom. It's choosing to follow Christ, no matter the cost, and to make one's body "a living sacrifice, holy and acceptable unto God" (Rom. 12:1).

While there are differing viewpoints on exactly what the divorce rate in America is, I don't think that anyone would disagree that it's too high. Combined with the general denigration of sex itself, many simply forego marriage altogether and opt for cohabitation. The logic goes that, "Since marriage is just a piece of paper, then what's the harm if we love each other? Besides, it's safer. We don't have to 'consciously uncouple' if it doesn't work out. We can move out and go our separate ways."

If sex isn't just another bodily function, then marriage isn't just another "relationship." When a man and a woman are joined as husband and wife, it isn't just an action of the community or even the state. God himself joins the couple. "What God has joined together, let not man separate." There are no qualifiers about how good of a match it is, whether the couple are making a mistake, or whether they even "love" each other. God joins them. This happens in every marriage, every time.

Homosexual "marriage" isn't

At first glance, it appears that I have overplayed my hand. Some might argue that if God joins two homosexuals together, then who are we to deny that reality? The answer is that God does not join people contrary to his foreordained design. Remember, the body has a marital meaning, reflecting the love that Christ and the church should have for each other. So-called "homosexual marriage" twists the meaning of marriage by making it insular. If two men, then it implicitly says that God the Trinity doesn't care enough to get outside of himself and share his life with mankind. If two women, it implies that humanity can find its fulfillment within itself, thank you very much.

So how do we deal with homosexuals? With hearts of gold and backbones of steel. We need to first remember that most theological attempts to explain away the scriptures and historic Christian understanding on this issue spring from the same roots of unbelief that have undermined other Christian teachings, such as the nature of God, the deity of Christ, and the resurrection. At its root, this is an issue of unbelief and spiritual warfare. "We do not wrestle against flesh and blood, but against ... the spiritual forces of evil in the heavenly places" (Eph. 6:12).

We also need to understand that, for a practicing homosexual to follow Christ, we may be asking him to end a union with a person about whom he cares very deeply. Even when it's twisted in such a manner, you can't persistently give yourself to someone sexually and not form a deep connection. In our current legal climate, such people may have legal relationships that include children. We can expect not only the normal mess we see in a heterosexual divorce, but also the full force of a community against us, which will undoubtedly blame us for unnecessarily breaking up a happy home. However, the Scriptures are clear, and "the cross is ruthless."[12]

12   Rosario Butterfield, https://www.thegospelcoalition.org/article/love-your-

What about a homosexual who longs for marriage and family, even if it's with someone of the same sex? We need to acknowledge that there is a licit element to his desires. Humans are made for fellowship with other people. It is a natural and laudable desire to care for and nurture another person. However, love must be according to form, or it's not true love. One of the lost arts of our age is a true, deep, same-sex friendship. Two people can deeply love and care for each other without having sex. Adults can pour their lives into children outside of marriage. It may not be easy, but it is possible.

God might be gracious enough to change a homosexual's desire. It has happened, and we shouldn't be embarrassed to proclaim this. "With God all things are possible" (Mat. 19:26). With our boldness, we also need to be humble and forthright enough to admit that sometimes — perhaps most of the time — God calls homosexuals to lifelong celibacy. If the church needs celibates, then doesn't this make sense?

Jesus promises to provide for our needs. Often, we view this in a purely material light, and while God does grant us daily bread, his provision for us is much more than that. As an introvert, I must confess that, many times, God has made provision for my social and emotional needs — which I have proceeded to spurn with one excuse or another. I have also often had to confess that what I thought I needed and what I actually needed were not perfectly aligned.

Some homosexuals insist that there's nothing wrong with them, and that they're perfectly happy as they are. Others — more, I suspect, than the world wants to admit — hate it and don't see any way out. They may have tried everything they can think of from conversion therapy to "praying the gay away," yet the desires persist. They ask, "If this is a sin, why do I want it so badly?" Some have simply concluded that God's solution for homosexuals is to let them get married like heterosexuals.

However, God's solution to all disordered desires, same sex attractions included, is either to change our desires or give us the grace to resist them. In keeping with our romantic/existentialist philosophy, rather than conforming our desires to reality, our society insists on trying to force reality to conform to our desires by redefining what marriage is. One of the arguments for redefining marriage is that rejecting someone's sexual behavior is to reject him as a person on an irrational basis, like rejecting different ethnicities because of said ethnicity. The standard rejoinder from evangelicals is to deny that sexuality takes such a central role in human personhood.

I think that, in our zeal to defend the truth, we end up missing it. Remember, sexual shame was the first recorded result of the first human sin. While this is undoubtedly an example of the body trying to express a truth beyond what it is capable,[13] why sexuality? What does Adam say when God calls him after eating the fruit? "I heard...you...and I was afraid, because I was naked..." (Gen. 3:10). Why mention nakedness? Why not say something along the lines of, "I disobeyed your command and ate the fruit"? Even granting Adam's desire to shift the blame to Eve, why does he blurt out, "I'm naked" instead of, "She did it first"? (I have young children. I've seen this many times.) The reason is that sexuality is indeed a crucial aspect of our beings. If we are bodies, doesn't it follow that sin should work from the inside out? If it affects the heart first, the things closest to the heart will manifest first (see Mat. 15:19). Even in a culture that denies the necessity of marriage, it's widely accepted that sexual behavior shows us at our most vulnerable and open.

Is it the most central aspect of who we are? No, but it is one of the most powerful longings we have as humans. Not only that, but our masculinity and femininity find proper expression, in part, in heterosexual, marital, sexual activity.

---

13 See C.S. Lewis's essay "Transposition" found in *The Weight of Glory*.

So why? Why would God allow people to have such powerful desires and then tell them not to indulge in them? Ultimately, for the same reason he preserves all of us through our besetting sins, sexual or not:

> But we have this treasure in jars of clay, to show that the surpassing power belongs to God and not to us. We are afflicted in every way, but not crushed; perplexed, but not driven to despair; persecuted, but not forsaken; struck down, but not destroyed; always carrying in the body the death of Jesus, so that the life of Jesus may also be manifested in our bodies. (2 Cor. 4: 7-10)

Before we move on, we need to make the problem worse.

Sex isn't ultimately about the body — even when hormones are raging

> But I say to you that whoever looks at a woman to lust for her has already committed adultery with her in his heart. (Mat. 5:28, NKJV)

We Christians have read over this so many times that we may be immune to the shock of it, but an unbeliever might ask a pointed question. "How is that even possible? Isn't adultery, **by definition**, committed bodily?" Committing adultery is merely the fruition of lust (Ja. 1:15). It begins with sinful desire. It begins when, instead of seeing a woman as a fellow human created in the image of God, whose very body is the complement of mine in proclaiming the truth of God, I see her as a means for my own gratification. Harking back to John Paul II, I want to use her instead of loving her. So, physical adultery, although serious, is merely an advanced symptom of a very pernicious disease.

No treatment of this subject would be complete without mentioning the modern scourge of pornography. Even if we had no other scriptural support, Christians should oppose it based on Matthew 5:28 alone. Yes, the social ills are many and better documented all the time,[14] but we need something more fundamental than public policy choices. That something isn't even the warning of, "You shall not commit adultery" (Ex. 20:14), or even Jesus's further warning that we can commit "non-contact" adultery.

What we need is purity of heart. Our desires need to be radically renovated. "Christ's words spoken in the Sermon on the Mount are not a call hurled into emptiness."[15] Jesus doesn't just give us moral commands. He also gives us the Holy Spirit to renovate our desires. That's why public policy is insufficient; while it's necessary, it lacks the soul-transforming power of the Spirit. For those who follow him, he gives the grace of sexual self-control (Gal. 5:23) and possibly marriage as a means for that self-control (Prov. 18:22).

While marriage is partially ordained in the present state as a remedy for lust, it is possible to transfer that lust to the spouse. John Paul II ignited an international firestorm when he pointed out that, "A man can commit such adultery 'in the heart' even with his own wife, if he treats her **only** as an object for the satisfaction of drives."[16] John Calvin also enjoins sexual modesty by forbidding "unrestrained indulgence."[17] He calls for sexual temperance between spouses. Interestingly, he approvingly quotes Ambrose's condemnation of the man who is immodest in sexual intercourse as "committing adultery with his wife."[18]

What to do? The battle begins in the heart and the mind. Given that sexual sin strikes us near the core of our being, we

14 Please see *Pornified: How Pornography is Transforming Our Lives, Our Relationships, and Our Families* by Pamela Paul, and *Your Brain on Porn: Internet Pornography and the Emerging Science of Addiction* by Gary Wilson for further details.
15 *Theology of the Body* 46:5.
16 *Theology of the Body* 44:3. Emphasis not in original.
17 *The Institutes of the Christian Religion*, 2:8:44.
18 Ibid.

should expect the battle to be most intense here. This is one of the easiest sins to enjoy the pleasure of — for a little while (Heb. 11:24-26). It's always right there. Like a drug addiction, it generally follows the pattern C.S. Lewis describes as, "An ever-increasing craving for an ever-diminishing pleasure."[19]

I suspect that part of the reason why we produce and consume so much pornography is due to the hyper-individualism of American culture. Remember, sex is the ultimate expression of human communion. It's a fellowship of persons, a community of two. Sexual sin offers a counterfeit of true fellowship; it falsely promises pleasure independent of God. Does this mean that God is anti-pleasure? No, he invented it! One of the devil's greatest lies is that God's a dour killjoy (see Ps. 16:11).

To the world, it looks like God is holding something good back from us for no good reason. They claim that to ask people in modern society to go without sex, not remarry after a divorce, or even deny their proclivities towards same-sex unions meets H.L. Menken's definition of a Puritan as someone who is deathly afraid that someone, somewhere, is happy.[20] However, is it not the height of insanity to not listen to an omniscient being who has our best interests at heart? Surely we can see how many broken homes, bodies, and souls the sexual revolution has left in its wake. How much wreckage must we who claim the name of Jesus Christ both cause and endure before we listen to what he says?

> Cast away from you all the transgressions
> that you have committed, and make yourselves
> a new heart and a new spirit! Why will you die,
> O house of Israel? (Eze. 18:31)

---

19 *The Screwtape Letters*, pg. 44.
20 Paraphrased from H.L. Mencken, *A Mencken Chrestomathy* (Alfred A. Knopf, NY, NY 1949), pg. 624.

Chapter 5

What God Has Joined Together, Let Not Man Put Asunder

Alien is widely considered one of the best horror or science-fiction movies ever made. One reviewer has described it as a "haunted house in space." The protagonists aren't skilled warriors, brilliant scientists, or otherwise exceptional. They're "truck drivers in space" who are just trying to get their cargo to its destination and get home. The titular alien is perfectly designed to kill. Strong, stealthy, and fast, its mouth is jammed full of spiked teeth, it has razor-sharp claws, a spiked tail, and highly acidic blood which could eat through the ship's hull. This last characteristic effectively prevents the woefully underarmed crew from killing it. All attempts to capture the alien fail, and the tension rises as the crew is killed one by one.

Alien also has an unsettling undertone that I never noticed until I watched an interview with one of its screenwriters. His stated goal was to make every man in the audience squirm.

Horror films must do this on some level, and *Alien*'s screenwriters decided to do it by loading the film with Freudian sexual imagery. If you've ever seen the film, consider that the ship the alien eggs inhabit is shaped like a complete set of ovaries, fallopian tubes, and uterus. I won't dwell on the rest of the film except to note that the infamous birth scene is quite explicit in its use of phallic imagery. Taken together, this made *Alien* one of the best executed pieces of perversion that I've ever seen. The film took the sexual act, something that God designed to give life to all involved, and twisted it to bring death.

Given that all art is a product of its time, what does *Alien* say about our culture? We fear babies. They bring a kind of death. That idea would not have even been possible any earlier in world history. *Alien* was made in 1979, in a post-abortion, post-contraception, second-wave feminist America. Sex without consequence was the goal, and abortion was justified and legalized to liberate women to live free, unencumbered lives and to spare children from unnecessary misery. Feminism had mutated from equal standing before law to making men and women exactly alike except for anatomy. If men can have sex and just walk away, then women should be able to as well.

The West, especially America, has a weakness for accepting anything couched in the language of "freedom." Add in some "equality," and we just can't help ourselves, and that's exactly what the sexual revolution did. Men and women should be treated exactly alike, biology be damned. "Make love, not war," was one of the catchphrases. Sex had an almost mystical quality to it.

From the world's perspective, there was one small "problem" with that. Sex could result in children, which were perceived as a great hindrance to "freedom" and "equality." Since abortion was still illegal in most states, the emphasis moved to preventing conception in the first place so children wouldn't have to be aborted later.[1] With the advent of the birth control pill, the sexual revolution achieved its goal of having its cake and eating it too. They were ever copulating, but never conceiving (except when they did, but that's what abortion was for). Joni Mitchell's lumps of billion-year-old carbon were finally free.

However, fifty years on, the sexual revolution has experientially discovered the partial-truth of philosopher Jean-Paul Sartre's maxim that "man is condemned to be free."[2] Collegiate "hook-up" culture has left many wondering if there's something better. They've been told that they're the product of evolution, that the morality of their parents is dead, and that "personal peace and affluence"[3] is the highest goal. If sex helps you achieve personal peace, then go for it. On the other hand, since the body has a marital meaning, and the sexual act has meaning within that framework, we need to review what sex is for. First, mutual help of husband and wife. Second, preventing sexual sin, and third, procreation. In marriage, all come together.[4]

To paraphrase T.S. Elliot, we need to know what something is before we can say what it's for. In the case of marriage, what it is and what it's for are the same thing at their root: marriage is a physical demonstration of a spiritual reality about how God relates to his people. God, as the Nicene Creed reminds us, is "the giver of life." God is generous, giving and sustaining every life on this planet, from humans all the way down to single-cell amoebas. If God is generous and life-giving, and if marriage is supposed to be an analogy of that generous life-giving, that leads us to some conclusions that will make us very uncomfortable. At

---

1   Then-US President Barack Obama suggested as much in his Spring 2009 commencement speech at Notre Dame University when he called for pro-lifers to work with pro-abortionists to "reduce unintended pregnancies." http://time.com/4336922/obama-commencement-speech-transcript-notre-dame/, last accessed June 3, 2019.
2   *Existentialism is a Humanism*, p 29
3   Francis Schaeffer, *A Christian Manifesto* (Crossway Books, Wheaton, Ill 1982), pg. 77.
4   This division comes from the 1920 *Anglican Book of Common Prayer*, Liturgy of Matrimony.

the root of our societal problems with marriage and sexuality is a faulty idea about what bodies are for. Part of what bodies are for is to beget children. In the 20th century, we had unprecedented success separating sex and procreation, entering author Aldous Huxley's *Brave New World*.

Yes, get consent, but you need more than that

Before delving too far into this topic, we should address one of its underlying assumptions. Western, and more particularly, American, culture is built on the idea of mutual consent. From informed consent paperwork for medical procedures to college consent codes for student sexual conduct, the background assumption is that if everyone involved in an act consents to it with full possession of his mental faculties, practically anything goes.

Some caution must be used here. Consent **is** very important. The very classification of a sexual act as an assault or even as rape explicitly states that the victim did not consent to the act. To borrow a mathematical expression, in sex, consent is necessary, but not sufficient. Especially in modern American collegiate contexts, consent often means that the parties merely consent to use each other. This is part of the reason why collegiate and governmental efforts to fight sexual assault by insisting on and meticulously defining consent will inevitably fail. Why isn't mutual sexual consent enough? Paul deals with this when he warns that, "...whoever sins sexually, sins against his own body" (1 Cor. 6:18, NIV).

At first glance, this seems like a strange thing to say. Aren't there other ways that I could sin against my body? Overeating, self-cutting, and illicit drug use are only a few, but there's something unique about sex. If we assume that the body has a marital meaning, this suddenly starts making sense. If I, as a man, am designed to mate with a woman in wedlock, then anything other than that misuses my body. Even extra-marital heterosexual sex is a violation of the meaning of the body, because the body is intended "for the Lord" (1 Cor. 6:13).

How is it intended for the Lord? Paul tells us in Ephesians 5 that it mirrors the union between Christ and the church. We've already looked at the unitive and the fraternal aspects of marriage, but what about the generative? Can it be separated from the other two?

Rethinking artificial contraception

Officially, Roman Catholicism is the only major church that outright condemns artificial contraception. The fundamental rationale is that sex has two purposes. First, the union of husband and wife (mutual help and prevention of sexual sin), and second, procreation. The argument runs that these purposes were united by God and cannot be separated by man "on his own initiative."[5]

When Catholic teaching on the matter was re-affirmed in 1968, most Protestants chuckled to themselves and went right on doing what they had been doing. Now, contraception is an issue that Protestants don't think about. It's just assumed that married couples will use it. Why? Luther[6] and Wesley[7] were against it, and Calvin also disapproved the practice.[8]

Their disapproval was based on this passage:

>   ... Judah took a wife for Er his firstborn, and

---

5   *Humanae Vitae* 12.
6   Martin Luther, *Luther's Works*, ed. Jaroslav Pelikan, translated by Paul D. Pahl (Concordia Publishing House, St. Louis, MO 1965), 7:20-21.
7   John Wesley, *Commentary on Genesis 38:7*, although this is unclear from the context, especially given Wesley's *A Word to Whom it May Concern*, where he attacks masturbation.
8   John Calvin, *Commentary on Genesis 38*. While his onus is on "a woman in some way [driving] away the seed out of the womb, through aids..." it's reasonable to assume that he would also neither condone condoms nor hormonal contraception..

her name was Tamar. But Er, Judah's firstborn, was wicked in the sight of the Lord, and the Lord put him to death. Then Judah said to Onan, "Go in to your brother's wife and perform the duty of a brother-in-law to her, and raise up offspring for your brother." But Onan knew that the offspring would not be his. So whenever he went in to his brother's wife he would waste the semen on the ground, so as not to give offspring to his brother. And what he did was wicked in the sight of the Lord, and he put him to death also. (Gen. 38:6-10)

Ancient Jewish and Christian commentators agreed that Onan's sin was a crime against nature, a violation of the sexual act. Modern commentators counter by observing that Onan's motivation was to avoid providing his dead brother with an heir. In that case, Onan would receive the double portion of his father's estate, so what angered God was not his practice of *coitus interruptus* (not masturbation, the traditional interpretation), but his greed. Therefore, the logic goes, it wasn't the contraceptive act *per se*, but the motivations behind the act that brought down God's wrath.

Our mistake as moderns is separating the two. The act was the poisoned fruit of an evil heart (Mat. 12:35). He contracepted for monetary reasons. He was not being generous. This also had the "fringe benefit" of allowing Onan to continue to have sex with Tamar, which would normally be forbidden, since she was still considered his sister-in-law. He could get the fun and the money to go with it, and if it left Tamar destitute, that was her problem.

Is this ancient story even relevant today? Absolutely. Why do we contracept? So we can have sex and not conceive children. If we were only concerned about not conceiving children, we could just not have sex and be done with it, and by "we," I mean

Christians. We shouldn't expect the world, which doesn't have the Holy Spirit, to be chaste. Like the world and Onan, we Christians want the fun without dealing with the children that the fun brings. Again, why? We should note here that the "body speaks a 'language' of which it is not the author."[9] It's one thing to say, "I love you," with the mouth, but what does artificial contraception say bodily?

Our bodies express what we really mean

Answer: "I want to use you. I want you to give me pleasure, and then be done with it. I don't want to deal with anything or anyone that might come of our union." To some, that might sound harsh. I submit it sounds harsh because it describes a harsh attitude. It's also the attitude that some men take towards the mothers of their children when pressuring them to have an abortion. We need to face up to the fact that, in most situations, abortion is used as after-the-fact birth control, either because the primary method "failed" or because it **is** the primary method.[10] Some might take offense at being compared to abortionists, but isn't the same mindset behind contraception and abortion? Aren't both an attitude of "I want sex but not babies?" Isn't the abortionist simply willing to go further to achieve his end?

If the body speaks a language of which it is not the author, what else does artificial contraception say? It's an embodied lie. What's the lie? The sexual act says, "I give myself to you entirely, and I'm committed to you," while contraceptive use explicitly holds something back, our reproductive capabilities. We're all

9   *Theology of the Body* 104:7. In the present author's opinion, this is the most critical sentence in *Theology of the Body* and crystalizes its teaching.
10   Rachel K. Jones, Lori Frohwirth, and Ann M. Moore, "More than poverty: disruptive events among women having abortions in the USA," found at http://jfprhc.bmj.com/content/39/1/36#T3, last accessed June 29, 2017. Table 3 of this document states that 51% of women surveyed in 2008 were using some contraceptive method during the month in which they conceived. Please also see Ms. Jones's follow up study at https://www.contraceptionjournal.org/article/S0010-7824(18)30003-9/fulltext, last accessed March 18, 2020.

familiar with embodied lies in other areas of our lives. The man who shakes your hand and then double-crosses you on a deal lied in two ways. First, he lied with his mouth, and then he embodied that lie, ratifying it.

Artificial contraception intentionally breaks a working body system. The reproductive system is meant to conceive babies and bring them to birth. Even the most hard-core evolutionist will agree with that assertion. No other body system is intentionally broken like this. Even with gastric bypass, the idea is to reduce the amount of food that the stomach can hold, not keep the stomach from digesting, and that's a last-ditch effort to accomplish what diet and exercise couldn't.

Yes, sex is intended for pleasure, but mere pleasure is not its end and meaning. It's meant, when done properly, to bring joy to both husband and wife. It's also meant to point both to the glories of Christ.[11] I don't want to minimize or downplay that. But it's meant for more, and we Protestants have been guilty for years of downplaying the generative aspect and playing up the unitive. In more recent Protestant works, the focus has more crassly been on pleasure.[12] Catholics repeatedly point out that no Protestant denomination approved contraception before the 1930 Anglican Lambeth conference. The unspoken question they keep asking us is, "If you thought it was a sin before, why don't you now?"

It would be one thing if we would answer the question adequately. As a rule, we don't. Every Protestant defense of contraception that I've ever seen fails on at least one level to answer the Catholic Church's assertions. Why? I suspect that, while we don't want to say it outright, we think their position is silly, intransigent, and unrealistic. It's easier to wave it off with a *Sola Scriptura* than deal with what they're saying. In

---

11   See John Piper, Chapters 1 and 2 of *Sex and the Supremacy of Christ*.
12   For example, see *The Act of Marriage* by Tim and Beverly LaHaye and *Intended for Pleasure* by Ed and Gay Wheat.

a move of breathtaking arrogance, some claim that the church was wrong all along, and now we've become more enlightened.

A scriptural fast you may never have noticed

When discussing contraception, Christians like to quote, "Do not deprive one another" (1 Cor. 7:5). That's correct, but not the full sentence. The full sentence is, "Do not deprive one another, except perhaps by agreement for a limited time, that you may devote yourselves to prayer; but then come together again, so that Satan may not tempt you because of your lack of self-control." In the fuller context, Paul calls Christians to sexually fast. Like a food fast, we are to replace sex with prayer.

This is the exact opposite of modern Protestant thinking. One popular Protestant work on fighting lust suggests having frequent sex as a counter-measure.[13] I affirm that one of the purposes of marital sex is "the prevention of fornication and uncleanness."[14] Sex is a good thing, but like all things, it can be put to unholy uses.

The parallels between sex and food are striking when considering fasting. We fast, not because the things that we fast from are bad, but to show that something — rather, someone — is better. We can only truly find the goodness of sex and food through Christ. We are saying to the world that there is someone whose presence is better than eating or having sex. If this is radical with respect to food, consider how much more radical it is in our culture with respect to sex!

Fasting is making somewhat of a resurgence as a spiritual discipline, and that is a good thing. We need to train our bodies that "Man shall not live by bread alone, but by every word that comes from the mouth of God" (Mat. 4:4, quoting Deut. 8:3). We

13   Fred Stoker and Steve Arterburn, *Every Man's Battle*, (Waterbrook Press, Colorado Springs, CO, 2000) pg. 148-149.
14   1920 *Anglican Book of Common Prayer*, Liturgy of Matrimony.

need God more than food or sex. If that's true, and Christians ought to agree that it is, why have we never heard any teaching on the sexual fast?

Many of the principles of food fasting apply. For example, Paul explicitly states that we must devote ourselves to prayer during this fast. Not having sex for the sake of not having sex not only misses the point but is stealing from our spouse to a certain extent. Fasting without prayer is what Eastern Orthodox Christians refer to as a demon's fast: "...demons never eat, but they never pray."[15] If prayer is important while on a food fast, how much more so during a sexual one?

Catholicism and Eastern Orthodoxy have very prescribed rhythms of food fasting. While we may not impose those from without, sexual fasting is written into our very nature, if we'll pay attention to it. If we want to be more like Christ — who fasted sexually his entire life — we need to follow our rhythms.

Christians like to quote, "I can do all things through him who strengthens me" (Phil. 4:13) when we're in the middle of a marathon or facing a crunch at work, but do we believe it? Do we really believe that God can grant us grace to not only endure, but thrive in — no, **because of** — a sexual fast? If we can't say no and stick to it, does our yes mean anything?

Isn't this going just a bit too far?

Some might argue that I'm stretching this too far. After all, there is no Bible verse that says, "Thou shalt not use artificial contraception." Most modern Protestant theologians would argue that this is a matter left to the individual conscience, and we shouldn't make a blanket rule.[16] This, as mentioned

15   Fr. Stephen Freeman, "A Modern Lent," found at https://blogs.ancientfaith.com/glory2godforallthings/2019/03/29/a-modern-lent-2/, last accessed April 10, 2019.
16   For example, see Wayne Grudem, *Systematic Theology* (Zondervan, Grand Rapids, MI, 1994) pg. 133.

earlier, is an inadequate understanding of *Sola Scriptura*. If a teaching can be "by good and necessary consequence...deduced from Scripture," that teaching is just as valid on us as if it was explicitly stated in Scripture.

It might also help if we start in our current cultural situation and work backwards. How did we even get to a state where we could possibly consider two men in a sexual relationship to be "married"? How could we just blithely throw away the teaching of the Bible and the historic witness of the church about the impropriety of homosexual unions? Because we had already redefined marriage. We redefined it from a covenantal, iconographic union intended for mutual fellowship and fruitfulness to a strictly romantic, feelings-based relationship. That gets us to no-fault divorce. If you can "fall in love," then it becomes just as easy to fall out of it.

A second redefinition was that, before the advent of oral contraception, it was assumed that healthy marriages and sexually healthy couples would produce children. (This does not include infertility. I am writing here about physically and spiritually healthy marriages.) Now, whatever the reasons for not having children, which are almost always monetarily based, Christians overwhelmingly accept artificial contraceptive use to plan their families.[17] If marriage is a feelings-based relationship that's about my self-actualization, then, if children don't actualize me, I shouldn't have them. Classically, Christians called this sort of thinking "sloth."

Further, Christians started separating methods from ethics.[18] They argue that, "Even if you reject oral contraceptives because of their abortifacient properties, other methods are as valid, since a fertilized egg isn't harmed. Besides, what's the problem with

17   R. Jones and J. Dreweke, "Countering Conventional Wisdom: New Evidence on Religion and Contraceptive Use," (Guttmacher Institute, NY,NY, 2011) referenced at https://www.guttmacher.org/fact-sheet/contraceptive-use-united-states, last accessed April 3, 2017.
18   *Theology of the Body* 124:4-6.

artificial methods, since periodic abstinence also tries to have sex and not conceive? Don't natural and artificial contraception just try to do the same thing?"

To see the absurdity of the "there's no difference between artificial and natural contraception if the end goal is the same" argument, let's examine an increasingly common, but related, transplantation of it. As I write this, Colorado and Washington, D.C. are considering implementing euthanasia laws. What's the argument? We're only going to allow this in cases where people are terminally ill. "They're going to die anyway, so we should mercifully help kill them." So we're going to put Grandma down like her dog Fifi? The ends do not justify the means, and the Apostle Paul condemns those who "say 'Let us do evil that good may come'" (Rom. 3:8, NKJV).

Other theologians, seeing the "Fifi dilemma," attempt to make the argument that, while married couples overall should be open to children, that doesn't necessarily mean that every sexual act should be open to it. A moment's reflection will show the absurdity of this line of reasoning. If I can separate sex from procreation, why can't I separate it from faithfulness? If sex can be just an expression of love, I can "love" another woman, can I not? Doesn't this implicitly condone premarital sex? If no serious Christian would accept this argument, how is the "overall openness to life" argument any different?

Others object that we have fulfilled the creational mandate. We have been fruitful, and we have multiplied. To hear some, we have multiplied too much, because the Earth has too many people right now. First, who decides that the Earth has too many people? Isn't it ultimately God who opens the womb and grants us food? We must be careful of giving ourselves too much credit. Second, who says that we can stop procreating? That would be analogous to arguing that we won't have to evangelize once the church is established in every people group. The Great Commission is in force until Jesus returns — and so is the creational commission. Seem far-fetched? If marriage is an analogy of Christ's relationship to the church, it shouldn't.

Does this mean that I must have my own football team? No. Prudence is required. Having more children than is wise is the complementary vice to intentionally not having any at all. Couples must understand their limits, whether energy, space, or material resources, and prayerfully discern God's will.[19] Some couples will conceive as many children as they can. They are a rare and special group. Most won't.

Virtue may be difficult, but it brings joy

My wife let me in on a secret that I wouldn't have guessed. She told me that one of the things that attracts her to practicing sexual fasts is that she doesn't feel used. Sadly, too many men are willing to use their wives to have their fun, and artificial contraception makes it that much easier.[20]

What is the point of the Christian life? I submit that it's "to be conformed to the image of his Son [Christ]" (Rom. 8:29). How does that happen? First, through the inworking of the Holy Spirit. Without him, the whole endeavor is in vain, but that doesn't mean that we sit around and do nothing. Realizing that he works in, through, and with our efforts (with a lot more that we have little or nothing to do with), we engage in spiritual disciplines. After all, this is war (see 2 Tim. 2:2-4).

If we have the Holy Spirit, we should show its fruits, and one list of those is given in Galatians 5:23-24: "Love, joy, peace, patience, kindness, goodness, faithfulness, gentleness, self-control." Sexual fasts focus on the last one in the list, self-control. "Self-control" is a truncated translation of the

19 *Theology of the Body* 121:5, referencing *Humanae Vitae* 10.
20 *Humanae Vitae* 17.

Greek word ἐγκράτεια, (pronounced eng-krat'-i-ah). A fuller translation might read, "self-control, especially regarding sexual matters."[21]

Does using artificial contraception trend toward making us more holy or less holy? When contracepting, does it help we men to "love our wives as [our] own bodies" (adapted from Eph. 5:28)? Does it help us "abstain from the passions of the flesh" (1 Pet. 2:11), or does it tend to make peace with them? Does it work with the grace of God for "training us to renounce ungodliness and worldly passions" (Tit. 2:12)? Does it affirm or deny that "children are a heritage from the Lord" (Ps. 127:3)? Does it help us "fan into flame" (2 Tim. 1:6) the virtues of temperance or self-control?

Some might object that this is no one's business except mine and my spouse's. As Christians, we don't get to unilaterally dictate the terms of our sex lives. As Pastor John MacArthur points out, part of our fundamental identity in Christ is that of a slave.[22] We don't own ourselves, and we don't get to totally decide what to do with our bodies and when. If we are slaves to Christ (Rom. 1:1; Eph. 6:6; Col. 3:24; Phil. 1:1; Tit. 1:1; and 1 Pet. 2:16), and slaves must obey their masters in everything, then Jesus has a lot to say about our sex lives. Like eating and drinking (see 1 Cor. 10:31), we are also to have sex to the glory of God. As Westerners, this grates against our sensibilities. After all, "we have never been slaves of anyone" (Jn. 8:33, NIV).

One attribute of babies is inescapable: helplessness. Everything must be done for them except sleeping. (Oh, if only parents could sleep on behalf of their children, but I digress.) When examining the animal kingdom, this is unheard of outside of primates. Even for primates, the length of a human helpless

---

21   James Strong, *The New Strong's Complete Dictionary of Bible Words*, ed. John R. Kohlenberger III (Thomas Nelson Publishers, Nashville, TN, 1996), Greek Dictionary entry 1466. Also see *Theology of the Body* 53:5.
22   This is the central thesis of MacArthur's book *Slave: The Hidden Truth About Your Identity in Christ.*

period is so long that Stephen J. Gould once described human babies as "extra-uterine embryos."[23] Spend a week feeding, changing, clothing, feeding again, burping, clothing again, changing again, clothing again, carrying, rocking, feeding again, desperately trying to get it to sleep, and his statement becomes much more understandable.

Compared to the rest of the animal kingdom, this should strike us as strange. In chapter 2, I argued that man is the pinnacle of God's creation, his vice-regent in the world. If he's the highest physical lifeform, then why did God make him so helpless when a baby, especially when compared with other species? For example, horse colts can stand within minutes after birth and can run the next day. Shouldn't his period of helplessness be shorter than all other species? Shouldn't he mature faster? Isn't this backwards?

I don't think that it is backwards. The helpless period isn't for the child as much as it is for the parents. It's divine training in learning how to love and care for difficult people. Babies may look cute and innocent, but when it's 4 a.m., he's already been up for two hours, and the alarm goes off at 6 a.m. to get ready for work, you will want to strangle your child — or worse.

What, then, are we doing to ourselves by foregoing children? We are forfeiting divine generosity training. This is **not** unselfishness training. Lewis observes that "unselfishness" often merely goes without something so someone else can have it, all the while resenting the other person for taking what the "unselfish" one wants.[24] This is the act without the attitude to go with it (2 Cor. 9:7).

Babies without sex

If contraception is the attempt to have sex without babies,

---

23   Quoted by Frederica Mathewes-Green in "Bodies of Evidence," *Touchstone*, June 2005.
24   C.S. Lewis, *The Weight of Glory*, p. 25

assisted reproductive technology[25] is the attempt to have babies without sex. It's merely the flip side of the contraception coin, and it too has brought bitter fruit with it. While artificial insemination has been around since the late 1800s, *in vitro* fertilization (IVF) is comparatively recent. The first child successfully born using the procedure, Louise Brown, was born in 1978. Since then, hundreds of thousands of babies have been conceived and born via IVF.

The brokenness of our bodies inevitably extends to our reproductive systems. Like all other medical treatments, we need to ask:

- What treatments are licit and why?

- How far should Christians be willing to go to have children naturally?

- What can we as the church do to help those who have sinned in this area?

In my experience, infertility can wreak havoc on a marriage. Both the husband and wife can not only experience the persistent frustration of a legitimate desire but also feelings of inadequacy on a fundamental level. While other physical impairments can certainly drive people into depression, infertility seems to be harder on people experiencing it. If the body does have a marital meaning, and if sexuality is near the core of our personhood, does this not make sense?

The purposes of sex are not separable, and the current reproductive free-for-all in the West shows us what happens when we do separate them. In a vicious feedback loop, our separation of sex and babies has furthered the decline of marriage. Once the gametes are separated from the sexual act,

---

25　While the broader accepted medical definition of assisted reproductive technology explicitly excludes artificial insemination (for example, see the World Health Organization's definition, found at https://www.who.int/reproductive-health/publications/infertility/art_terminology2.pdf?ua=1, last accessed May 15, 2019), I will include it for the purposes of this chapter.

we can master them like we master our own bodies. A large collection of short steps brought us where we are today. If artificial insemination is legitimate for a husband whose sperm is defective, why not get someone else's sperm if necessary? If a woman can conceive with another man's sperm, why does she need a husband at all? If a wife can get another man's sperm, why not get someone else's eggs if hers have a problem? If the eggs are fine, why not rent someone else's uterus if there's a problem with that instead? If couples can have their baby in another woman's uterus, what does it matter what sexes the parents are if you can get the gametes? If heterosexual couples can use assisted reproductive technology to have babies, why can't homosexual couples? Once we discard the idea that the body has a marital meaning and is merely something else for us to control, there's no rational argument against homosexual use of assisted reproductive technology. With marriage thus undermined, it reinforces the separation of sex from marriage and children, and around we go again.

Why "begetting" is important

"Beget" is a word that is little used outside the church. Per Merriam-Webster, "beget" means "to procreate as the father."[26] Having separated sex from procreation, we've lost the meaning of both. A subtle but highly important shift has taken place. Part of what bodies are for is begetting children, but when was the last time you heard anyone describe it that way? More often, don't we use the term "making babies"? The change in phrasing is more significant than we realize. As C.S. Lewis points out, "making" and "begetting" are two different things. Beavers make dams, but they beget beavers.[27] It's also part of the *Imago Dei*; God made the physical creation and the angels, but he eternally

---

26   https://www.merriam-webster.com/dictionary/beget, last accessed June 5, 2019.
27   *Mere Christianity*, pg. 138.

begets his own Son.

Assisted reproductive technology has received some help from the pro-abortion forces on this question. For years, the pro-abortion lobby has argued that the baby is essentially a parasite, which the mother has the right to expel if she so chooses. While that's a grossly inaccurate application of the term "parasite," it further allows them to argue that the mother essentially constructs a fetus, instead of the child being able to grow and develop in a self-directed manner when provided with the appropriate nutrients and conditions.[28] The position is consistent, however; if I can "make" a baby, then I can "unmake" it. The child is dehumanized either way.

The problem is that we've adopted an ends-justifies-the-means mentality. We've accepted the world's bargain that we can conceive children at any cost. The problem with that reasoning is that marriage does not automatically confer on couples the right to have children; it only gives them the right to try to conceive.[29] It also commoditizes children. We end up treating small people, who are God's image-bearers, like puppies or kittens.

So what can we do about infertility? We must remember two fundamental principles. First, medical treatments must treat the child/embryo as a person and care for it, as far as possible, just like any other person.[30] Second, a treatment is proper if it "seeks to assist the conjugal act either in order to facilitate its performance or in order to enable it to achieve its objective once it has been normally performed."[31] So surgeries to open blocked tubes, medications to restore proper hormonal functions, and even homologous artificial insemination (this procedure uses the husband's sperm for the process) may be proper.

---

28 For example, see https://www.youtube.com/watch?v=mf6tSW-BNLA, (beginning at approximately 29:50 of the clip), last accessed June 5, 2019.
29 Congregation for the Doctrine of the Faith, *Donum Vitae*, Section B, question 8.
30 *Donum Vitae*, 5.I, question 1.
31 *Donum Vitae*, 5.II.B, question 7.

Artificial insemination goes awry quickly when other gametes are used. While it may be useful for animals,[32] introducing a third party's gametes into a marriage or using the gametes of someone the mother may not even know fits John Paul II's criteria of using another person. The process of obtaining sperm is notorious for its crass use of the donors themselves. Colloquial stories abound of clinics allowing donors to use pornographic materials to "aid" the donation process. Sperm and eggs can be sold. Taking advantage of a man's need for money, the clinics virtually make him a prostitute. Women are often given anonymized information about the donors regarding intelligence, physical fitness, physical characteristics, etc. Growing up on a gentleman's farm, I've seen this done many times with respect to horses and dogs. To state the obvious, this does not befit a person created in the image and likeness of God.

The woman also demeans herself in the whole process. She completely abandons the marital meaning of her body. She doesn't give herself to her husband; instead, she takes what she regards as merely cells of interest from another man to get what she wants out of the transaction. She offers herself up to the clinic as just another meat machine to be manipulated per her desires.

In vitro fertilization and its unintended consequences

If the cause of infertility cannot be resolved, and if artificial insemination fails, the last resort to achieve pregnancy is in vitro fertilization. Gametes are first obtained from both the man and the woman. (For the woman, this tends to be much more labor intensive and painful.) They are then combined in a petri dish with a culture media for several days. The embryos are then evaluated for quality — i.e. which have the best chance of implanting and surviving. Since the procedure often generates multiple fertilized

---

32 *Donum Vitae*, 5.I, question 6.

eggs, some countries have guidelines for how many embryos can be placed in the woman based on her age and health. Unfortunately, the United States is not currently among them.

What happens to babies that aren't implanted? We must be careful of picking up the world's clinically detached language. The world calls them "excess embryos." If they are human persons, then they are deep-frozen babies. Since most clinics do not receive instructions on what to do with the leftover children, they languish in a frozen limbo. The U.S. Department of Health and Human Services (HHS) estimates that over 600,000 babies are currently deep-frozen.[33] Some estimate the number to be as high as 1,000,000.[34]

We have the same moral numbness to freezing very small babies that we do to killing them via abortion. We can't see them, so we don't think of it. Freezing a "zygote" or an "embryo" doesn't sound bad. Freezing a baby, on the other hand, reveals it for the callous act that it is. Our righteous indignation rises at the idea of children working in dangerous sweatshops. It's one thing for an adult to choose to be placed in a dangerous situation, but we revolt, and rightly so, at placing children in mortal peril without them even being able to give consent to it.

A solution that's almost as bad as the problem

What do we do with the frozen babies? We should encourage the mothers who helped conceive them to accept their children and attempt to carry them to term. Unfortunately, some women are not willing to do this for multiple reasons, and no amount of persuasion will convince them otherwise. At this point, and **only** at this point should we encourage other women to adopt and attempt to carry them to term.

33 https://www.hhs.gov/opa/about-opa/embryo-adoption/index.html, last accessed June 4, 2019.
34 Tamar Lewin, "Industry's Growth leads to Leftover Embryos, and Painful Choices," *New York Times*, June 17, 2015.

I admit that this is a bad solution. It could be objected that, if I'm so concerned about maintaining the link between sex and procreation, how can I ever support surrogacy for any reason? Unfortunately, when discussing frozen children, the link between sex and procreation has already been broken. The children have been conceived outside the sexual act, and many times, outside wedlock. This is analogous to adopting a child out of the foster care system. Obviously, everyone's first choice is to heal the home of origin so that the children can stay. Only when there is a reasonable assessment that the home cannot or will not be healed should we consider sending the children to live elsewhere permanently. Is surrogacy an ideal solution? No. However, it's better than allowing them to languish in a frozen limbo to await certain death upon thawing.

There are good groups doing good work to try to rescue such children, such as the Snowflake project and the National Embryo Donation center. However, we must admit that they're trying to make the best of a bad situation. Approximately one-fourth of these children do not survive the freezing/thawing process. Given HHS's estimate of 600,000 children in deep freeze, that implies that 150,000 babies are either dead already or will not survive the thawing process. For a country that regularly aborts over 1,000,000 babies a year, our consciences are so seared that we think nothing of slaughtering another few thousand in the thawing process.

There is a scene that was unfortunately cut from the film *Gattaca* which speaks powerfully to this situation. Genetic analysis performed just after birth shows that the main character, Vincent, has a 99% chance of dying by age 30 of a heart condition. His parents turn to science for their next child. Using an advanced form of IVF and genetic manipulation, they guarantee that the child will have hazel eyes, not have the same "flaw" as the brother, and a whole host of other "desirable" traits.

The geneticist has produced four healthy embryos, two boys and two girls. After selecting the one for implantation, the mother, obviously squeamish, asks what will happen to the others. The geneticist, sensing the question behind her question, responds:

> "Ahh...they are not babies, Maria, merely human possibilities. *(He brings the petri dish over to her for inspection.)* Smaller than a grain of sand. See?"

Sad though it is, I've never seen a better refutation of this than Horton the Elephant's, "A person's a person, no matter how small."[35] We in the anti-abortion camp have been saying this for years. Now, we're undercutting it by disposing of our "human possibilities" just like the world.

So babies for thee but not for me? The world's right — we are hypocrites.

---

35   Dr. Seuss, *Horton Hears a Who!* (Random House, Inc. NY,NY, 1982), pg.6.

Chapter 6

"More Human Than Human" or Not at All

One of my great-grandmothers was born in 1905 and died in 2006, just two months short of her 101st birthday. Shortly after the funeral, I thought over the changes she'd seen. In her lifetime, she saw the advent of the automobile, air travel, antibiotics, nuclear power, space travel, the discovery of DNA, organ transplants, the computer, satellites, then satellite television, the internet, mobile phones…that's a momentous list, and it just scratches the surface. The 20th century saw a level of technological advancement unparalleled in recorded human history. I'm writing this on a device that was inconceivable in 1905 — and it's already obsolete!

While the causes of the century of innovation are complex, its philosophy comes down to two fundamental beliefs. First, the laws of nature are unchanging and discoverable. Second, we can use science to develop technology to improve our lives. If God is not a god of disorder (1 Cor. 14:33, NIV), then we should expect the universe he created to be orderly.[1] Using technology to improve humanity's lot is part of how we exercise our vice-regency over the earth. I greatly appreciate the eradication of smallpox. I like air conditioning. The green revolution has enabled us to feed more people than even the most ardent opponents of Thomas Malthus would have dreamed possible.

So what does any of this have to do with our bodies? Everything. Just as we have sought to master the physical world and disease, we now seek to master our very selves. We now have an unprecedented level of medical technology that we can wield on our bodies. Combining such medical technology with the existentialist assertion that we impose our own meaning on the world and even ourselves leads to one of the biggest category mistakes in recorded history. We've mistaken our bodies for machines.

While some manifestations of this fundamental mistake may be new, the underlying errors of mistaking our bodies for machines are as old as the church itself. This is modern day Gnosticism spending billions of dollars attempting to make it happen. Ancient Gnostics, like their modern-day counterparts, believed that bodies are unimportant, even immaterial. If they are important, they are only important to the extent that they allow me to express the "real me," suggesting that physical reality is less real than our souls. Given the Enlightenment soil out of which empiricism springs,[2] this philosophical reversal is sadly ironic.

Sexual manipulation paves the way for other forms of bodily manipulation. While we didn't see it at the time because the technology hadn't matured, contraception led to abortion,[3]

---

1   Not everything in the universe is orderly, as the second law of thermody-namics attests. This will be dealt with in chapter 7.
2   Empiricism holds that we primarily know truth via our sense experience and is a central assumption of modern science. This is summed up in Yogi Berra's aphorism, "You can observe a lot by just watching."
3   Contrary to American popular opinion, the "right to privacy" was not in-vented for *Roe v. Wade*. It was established in *Griswold v. Connecticut*, which was used as a precedent for Roe. Griswold struck down the Comstock laws, which al-

abortion to artificial reproductive technology, artificial reproductive technology to the notion of "gay marriage," and "gay marriage" to the transgender movement.[4] If sexuality is near the core of our personhood, then it's not a far stretch to assert that, if we can manipulate our procreative powers, then everything else is fair game.

Transvestitism becomes transgenderism

The transgender movement is the most real-world manifestation of a movement called transhumanism. While transgenderism naturally arises from the sexual revolution, much of its intellectual capital has been borrowed by transhumanists. There are three major manifestations of transhumanism. First is the aforementioned transgender movement, which is front and center in the West right now. The second is a burgeoning cybernetic movement, mostly confined to Silicon Valley at the moment. Third is the "social robotics" movement, which is gaining money and momentum from research into artificial intelligence.

Transvestitism is as old as antiquity. Even the Mosaic law contains injunctions against cross-dressing (Deut. 22:5). While, before, it was only possible to dress and act like the opposite sex, medical technology now dangles the carrot of attempting to truly become a member of the opposite sex. Having separated the sexual act from procreation, Western philosophy is now attempting to separate sexual identity from biology.

The separation goes even further than that. Academics now maintain with a straight face that a biological male can really be a woman, and vice versa. We don't even need surgery. We

lowed states to outlaw contraception. Also see *Evangelium Vitae* 13, where John Paul II argues that the "contraceptive mentality" lies behind both contraception and abortion.

4   Rob Smith, interview with Tony Reinke, "Why did the transgender revolution catch us by surprise?" found at https://www.desiringgod.org/interviews/why-did-the-transgender-revolution-catch-us-by-surprise, last accessed December 6, 2019.

can simply insist that even though our bodies are one sex, our "gender" doesn't necessarily need to match. I can "identify" as a woman, even though I'm a biological male, or even some of both, according to the vague notion of "gender fluidity."

However, the exact opposite is true. "Identifying" as a different sex isn't identification at all. John's "lust of the flesh" (1 Jn. 2:16, KJV) "…brings with it an almost constitutive *difficulty in identifying oneself with one's own body.*"[5] If the meaning of the body is to make the spiritual visible and express love to other people, then the focus on the body as an end instead of a means to an end fails to embody (pun intended) that meaning. The problem with so-called "transgenderism" is that it confuses what God and human culture make clear. It's an embodied lie.

The notion of "gender" isn't new. It's a linguistic term that's long been used to classify words in other languages. Many languages use masculine and feminine gendered words, and some languages, such as Greek and German, have a third gender, neuter. Gender theorists, following the Existentialists, began using the word "gender" to refer to how we identify as people, male or female, and the term has rapidly worked its way into everyday conversation. We quickly run into problems, however, when we apply the concept of gender to people. "Gender" denies our intrinsic masculinity and femininity.

Replacing "sex" with "gender" allowed the world to argue that, since expressions of masculinity and femininity are relative to culture, and every culture in the world has clothing styles or practices that could be considered strange or even offensive outside their culture, how can we argue that there even is such a thing as "appropriate" clothing or expressions for men and women?

This is missing the forest for the trees. Clothing serves an iconographic function, pointing to a deeper truth. While clothing

5   *Theology of the Body* 29:5. Italics in original.

norms vary from culture to culture and are undoubtedly influenced by the physical environment as well, the fact that we are incarnated as men and women does not.

At this point, the world might shrug its shoulders and say, "So what?" The "so what" is that the drive to "re-engineer" ourselves won't stop at the sexual. While masculinity and femininity are part of what it means to be human, the most fundamental thing about all men and women is that we are bodies (and souls). However, masculinity and femininity are linked to bodies by biological sex. If I can rearrange my anatomy (at least in part) to appear to be a different sex, I have just assaulted the link. Once that is granted, there's no rational reason to forbid rearranging any other part of my body.

To put it bluntly, "transitioning" is simply impossible. While unnatural hormone levels may be forcibly induced, if the unnatural hormone treatments are stopped, the body will attempt to revert to its previous state. Even so-called "gender confirmation" surgery merely leaves a person mutilated in the vain hope that he can force his genitals to match his feelings. However, the ersatz genitalia have only the appearance, but not the function of the original.

To truly "transition," we would need to replace the appropriate chromosomes. That's genetic mutilation on a horrifying scale. While we've mapped the human genome, our understanding of what the genes do is woefully inadequate. Replacing one gene with another can have unforeseen and disastrous results, but replacing an entire chromosome's worth is practically guaranteed to leave a patient crippled for life — if he even survives the process.[6]

"Transitioning" is another example of sanitizing language to disguise what it refers to. What it refers to is the intentional mutilation of a perfectly functional body based on the desires or

6   While it is a work of fiction, Tyrell's warning to Batty in *Blade Runner* should give us pause. He mentions such a treatment that morphed into a virus, observing that the patient was "...dead before he left the table."

emotional distress of the patient. Undoubtedly, such emotional distress can be a serious, if relatively rare, problem. As anyone who's ever lived abroad can testify, "culture shock" can be debilitating. It's possible to be in a crowd of people and feel profoundly alone, separated from familiar places and people, immersed in unfamiliar or even incomprehensible customs. How much more distressing must it be to feel an even more profound sense of disconnection, a disconnection within one's self?

Every transitioning story can be boiled down to one thing: "I felt like my body's gender didn't match who I really was, so I transitioned." The details may differ, but the core is the same. No one who attempts to transition ever says, "I felt like God was calling me to transition, and, while it was hard, it's been worth it because I'm glorifying God." On one level, this should be a giant alarm that something has gone desperately wrong with the way we are made. On another level, we should not be surprised to find that indwelling sin works its way down to even disrupt our own incarnations. While such cases should be handled with gentleness and care, "transitioning" isn't the answer. The suicide rate before the surgery is as high as after.[7] The body isn't the problem: the soul is.[8]

Our bodies have meaning, and that meaning is to express love to God, one another, and the world that he has created. While warnings about meddling with one's physiology are valid and should be heeded, they don't address the problem at its deepest level. The problem is that "transitioning" attempts to turn the body's meaning on its head. Asserting that we will choose our own sexuality is a twisted expression of pride, the ultimate inordinate self-love. Jesus's warning is borne out that "whoever

---

7   Paul McHugh, "Transgender Surgery isn't the Solution" in the *Wall Street Journal,* May 13, 2016 (originally published June 12, 2014).
8   This does not include intersex situations, in which the normal chromosomal, gonadal, or anatomical developments do not happen. While such situations are thankfully rare, the medical treatment and pastoring of such people can be enormously challenging and are outside the scope of this work.

loves his life loses it, and whoever hates his life in this world will keep it for eternal life" (Jn. 12:25). The body isn't primarily meant for self-expression (although mediation does imply expression of some sort), but for self-gift, gift of a man and a woman, first to God, then others, manifested in fatherhood and motherhood.

A common rejoinder is that fatherhood and motherhood are moot for people who can't have children. The New Testament rejects this. Timothy is Paul's "son in the faith" (1 Tim. 1:2, KJV). Paul also considered the entire Galatian church to be his children (Gal. 4:19, where he also speaks of birth pains, a "female" experience). John writes to "my little children" (1 Jn. 2:1, 12, and 28). John Piper notes that "marriage is for making children...disciples of Jesus."[9] and while he's certainly correct, Paul, the single man, shows that spiritual fatherhood isn't limited to husbands only.

If the body has a marital meaning, we can't rearrange the body without obscuring the meaning. That goes not only for transgenderism and so-called "gender confirmation" surgeries, but for the next wave of body modifications, the attempted merger of the biological and the electronic.

Merging machines and men

For a consistent Darwinian evolutionist, humanity is now at a crossroads. From an evolutionary standpoint, if we have an opportunity to "improve" ourselves, we must take it to avoid stagnation and even extinction as a species. This is evolution on steroids; instead of being at the mercy of natural selection and random mutation, we'll take charge of the process and improve ourselves. Where Christians ask the question, "Is the human body a fit subject for technological manipulation?" — consistent Darwinists give an unqualified yes. If there's no ultimate

9   John Piper, *This Momentary Marriage* (Crossway Books, Wheaton, Ill, 2009), pg. 138.

designer, and Darwinian evolution holds that there isn't, it doesn't matter what we do.

While for a previous generation, such suggestions might conjure up unnerving images, such as the Borg from *Star Trek*, our discomfort is dismissed for various reasons. "Humans have used tools from time immemorial. It's even a trait that we share with other primates. What's the difference," the transhumanists ask, "between a smartphone in the palm of your hand and one in your head?"

The difference is design. We are created as persons, not things. Granted, we use devices, surgeries, and other treatments to rectify our physical ailments and even deformities. The use of glasses is a prime example. Even in the case of more severe problems, the end goal is to get back to normal vision, not enhance it. That's been the goal of the medical establishment for years. First, do no harm, then, as much as possible, get the patient back to his optimal state.

Some threads of science fiction warn us about "improving" ourselves. DC Comics's Cyborg, a member of the Justice League, has struggled since his first appearance with the sense that he is no longer fully human. Even though he has super strength, durability, sonic weapons, and enhanced vision, he would willingly trade it all to regain a fully healthy organic body. While he is shunned by society for being radically different, he himself has a difficult time connecting to others. Since his body is no longer a full body, his fraternal relationship to the rest of the world has somewhat broken down as well. He uses his enhanced abilities to fight supervillains but stands apart from the people he protects.

Why does he do this? The common description is that he's lost some of his humanity. While he hasn't lost the *Imago Dei*, and thus is still human, he does blur the line between a person and a thing. His body, "more machine now, than man,"[10] does not fully mediate his soul as it once did. He's not technically "superhuman"; he's an "assisted" human who would die without his cybernetic parts.

Why does it matter? After all, Cyborg is a fictitious character whose existence is still rooted firmly in science fiction. It's easy to dismiss him as merely the product of a comic book writer's over-active imagination. It matters because Cyborg is the latest manifestation of an ongoing theme in world literature, the chimera. While in previous ages, the mash-up was that of various animals such as a dragon, lion, and snake, H.G. Wells upped the ante with *The Island of Dr. Moreau*, merging animals with people. Modern genetics and microbiology have raised serious doubts about whether such mergers are even possible, so we've moved on to cybernetics.[11] The form may change, but the warning is still the same: this is unnatural and should be avoided. Cyborg, in a certain sense, examines the problems caused by such a union rather than merely assuming them as previous ages did.

Are our bodies ours to do with what we please? We should be suspicious of that mentality; "It's my body" is one of the rallying cries of the pro-abortion movement. This isn't just the genetic logical fallacy, but one of the underlying assumptions of their worldview. "I am the master of my fate: / I am the captain of my soul."[12] Christians, on the other hand, are commanded to offer up our "bodies as a living sacrifice, holy and acceptable to God" (Rom. 12:1). One of the ways that we do that is to stay in the office where God has assigned us (Jude 6).

What transhumanists are attempting to do, by their own admission, is bypass the mediatory functions of our bodies.

10   Obi-Wan Kenobi's description of Darth Vader in *Return of the Jedi*.
11   Modern immunology casts serious doubt on whether this is possible either. The human immune system would attempt to reject such devices as foreign objects, causing serious long-term problems.
12   William Ernest Henley, "Invictus" lines 15-16.

Remember, our bodies mediate our souls. One Silicon Valley CEO doesn't like "compressed communication" and believes that our brains should interface directly with each other for "uncompressed communication."[13] Removing the intermediary "compressed" layer won't improve interpersonal communication. First, compression sacrifices information quality for speed. Uncompressing a signal means that the signal takes longer to transmit. Second, even a mental image can't convey the experience it tries to describe. An adult may stand awestruck at the ocean shore or the Grand Canyon, while his petulant teenager may be bored and reaching incessantly for his phone, desperately wishing to be somewhere else. One may transfer his image to the other, but how can he possibly transfer the experience or the sense of awe? Furthermore, do we really want to share all our thoughts with others? If Twitter has proven anything, it's that our unfiltered thoughts are indeed "a fire, a world of unrighteousness" (Ja. 3:6).

In chapter 2, I argued that mankind serves as a bridge between the spiritual and the physical. We have access to God that the rest of the physical creation does not. The physical world is also God's gift to us, and we are God's gift to the physical world. What then happens if we try to bypass our bodies for direct interaction with each other and the physical world?

First, we abandon our post as God's vice regents. This brings us back to the primordial sin: "You will be like God." Until the incarnation, the Trinity existed only as spirit. Angels also exist as pure spirit. The Platonist notion of being free from the body has plagued the church since its inception.[14] Second, if the body has any sort of meaning, we can't just dismiss it as merely a temporary vehicle to house our souls.

---

13   Christopher Mims, "A Hardware Update for the Human Brain" in the *Wall Street Journal*, June 5, 2017.
14   This is a fundamental tenet of Gnosticism as well.

Option #2: Genetic modification

We also can't just dismiss it as a collection of spare parts. While one branch of transhumanism wants to make us cyborgs, another dreams of tinkering with our genetic and chromosomal structures to either fix what they argue are "design flaws" in the human body or enhance it. Doesn't this describe the eugenic dreams of the 19th and 20th centuries? The Nazis were after the master race, but they got their malignant ideas from the Americans and British. The Americans began with breeding, and the Germans merely took the philosophical justifications and used them to perform surgeries, mutilations, and outright genocide in pursuit of their goals. Even now, long after the horrors of Nazi medical experimentation were revealed, man is still trying in the 21st century with fetal stem cells.

Prosthetics, implants, and genetic engineering may still be the stuff of science fiction, but the drive to "upgrade" the human body will push us there. We're already trying to boost our physical performance (albeit illicitly) by using anabolic steroids. One Silicon Valley industry captain has openly called for people to improve themselves by becoming cyborgs.[15] He's put his money where his mouth is by founding Neuralink, whose ultimate goal is to connect neurodes into animals' and peoples' brains.

We need to take a step back and admit what we're doing: self-mutilation. This is how transgenderism helps transhumanism. If I can mutilate myself sexually, why can't I mutilate myself in other ways? We recognize the danger of self-mutilation when it accompanies emotional or mental disturbances. We try to get people help to stop the attempt to destroy themselves. Psychological conditions exist where people want to amputate a limb. They are also recognized for the mental disorders that they are.

---

15   http://www.cnbc.com/2017/02/13/elon-musk-humans-merge-machines-cy-borg-artificial-intelligence-robots.html, last accessed August 5, 2019.

Sex may currently be the only exception, but it won't be for long. The film *Blade Runner* expresses this with the Tyrell Corporation's motto: "More human than human." That sums up exactly what transhumanists are after. It's not enough to have airplanes; they want us to have wings and fly ourselves.

However, it never really works that way. As Tyrell himself acknowledges in the film, the candle might burn twice as bright, but it only burns for half as long. Microbiology and modern genetics teach us that even that maxim is over-optimistic when dealing with our DNA. When genetic codes go awry, the result is often that the candle burns half as bright for half as long at best. The list of known congenital genetic or chromosomal diseases is long: Tay-Sachs, Huntington's, cystic fibrosis, Down syndrome, spinal muscular atrophy, sickle cell anemia, and that doesn't even scratch the surface. It also doesn't include the genes that may predispose people to heart disease, cancers, mental illnesses, etc.

False gods ultimately disappoint, and technology is no exception

Admittedly, humanity made tremendous progress in fighting disease through the 20th century. Several of the aforementioned genetic disorders can now be managed more successfully so sufferers have a fuller life. Other diseases that were untreatable in 1900 can now be treated or even cured. Given this track record, transhumanists ask why we can't go for the ultimate goal: immortality. This is a major thrust of the modern transhumanist movement. We want to eliminate death. Whether uploading our consciousnesses into a massive computer[16] or physically keeping ourselves from dying, our unwarranted technological optimism leads us to think it's possible. Their argument is, "Why do we

---

16   Issac Asimov, "The Last Question" found in *The Complete Stories*, Vol. 1 (Broadway Books, NY, NY, 2001). This also appears throughout the thought of futurist/transhumanist Ray Kurzweil.

age at all? What if we could figure out what's going on and stop or even reverse it? We've made unimaginable medical progress during the 20th century, so why assume it will stop? If we can prevent disease, why can't we prevent death?"

We already know why people get old and die. It's a result of sin (see Genesis 3 and 6:3). That's not to say that every death is directly traceable to some specific sin or set of sins, although some are. Transhumanism, being an admittedly secular philosophy, doesn't even take the concept of sin into account. Spiritual problems cannot ultimately be remedied by physical means. A failure to even take the spiritual into account means that the transhumanist project does not have a full concept of what it means to be human and is thus doomed to failure from the beginning.

Yes, Christians can agree with transhumanists that death is a bad thing. We should work for healing and wholeness where we can by not using people. Death is a result of sin's curse. The good news of the gospel is that Jesus has already begun to reverse the effects of the creational curse. We Christians have a "Gospel of Life," to use John Paul II's term, to proclaim. Since there is no ultimate hope for defeating death apart from this gospel of life, this means that the transhumanists are ultimately on a fool's errand.

One of the things behind the drive to defeat death is the fact that an unregenerate man is kept a slave to his fear of death (Heb. 2:15). This fear will drive him to do terrible things in desperation to preserve his own life. Combine this with the implicit notion that man is merely a meat machine, and forcibly taking from others what someone thinks he needs becomes a very real possibility. Forget the children; I need the resources they might consume to improve myself. From an evolutionary standpoint, if sharks can eat their own young, why can't I? This is not as far-fetched as it sounds. For example, one billionaire has funded experiments that take blood from young donors and transfuse it into older recipients to see if it will either extend the recipients' lifespans or restore some of their vigor.[17] Chilling parallels to *Dracula* immediately come to mind.

Christians should not embrace death as a friend. This subject will be dealt with more in the next chapter, but because of our hope in a resurrected Christ, we should be able to face death with the courage that death does not have the final word and that Christ uses the horror of death as a gateway to everlasting life, a life that far exceeds what we have here and now.

Admittedly, transhumanism is a fringe movement right now, but transgenderism would have been considered a fringe movement ten years ago. At least in the USA, the forced recognition of homosexual unions as "marriage" allowed the transgender movement to step out of the shadows of the homosexual rights movement.[18] If the pattern holds, transhumanism is also waiting for its moment to step into the limelight.

Robots - driving science fiction to science reality

There will certainly be some who, for whatever reason, resist the drive to genetically or cybernetically modify themselves. There is a parallel pathway opening up. Robotics is investing huge efforts into making robots that look, talk, and act like humans. Gone are the days of *Lost in Space*'s clunky robot, or even *Star Wars*'s human-acting but robotic looking C-3PO. While industrial robots look nothing like humans and are explicitly designed for a particular task, those who design and build so-

---

17   https://www.theguardian.com/technology/2017/jun/30/peter-thiel-wolly-mammoth-back-to-life-donation, last accessed July 13, 2017.

18   Rob Smith, interview with Tony Reinke, "Why did the transgender revolution catch us by surprise?" found at https://www.desiringgod.org/interviews/why-did-the-transgender-revolution-catch-us-by-surprise, last accessed December 6, 2019.

called "social robots" are aiming for seamless integration with human society.

The advent of so-called "sexbots" is bringing this to the forefront. This is no longer science fiction. They are currently manufactured in China, and several media reports have surfaced of brothels that are using such robots to "service" their clientele. When examined from a utilitarian perspective, several "advantages" are immediately apparent. The robots can be customized within a limited range. They don't complain about being used or even beaten,[19] and they don't demand pay or benefits. They can be cleaned after each encounter, eliminating the need for sexually transmitted infection treatment.

However, the transhumanists now ask the question, "What makes a person a person?" Simone de Beauvoir famously argued that "One is not born, but rather becomes, woman".[20] Her philosophical descendants extended that assertion to men, giving birth (pun intended) to the transgender movement. The transhumanists now push it even further to hold that acting enough like a person makes a robot a person. Films like *Ex Machina* and *A.I. Artificial Intelligence* along with the HBO series *Westworld* are built on this assertion. Accompanying this idea is the implicit notion that the robots are similar enough to us that they have rights and cannot be treated however we please. They make sentience the criterion for human personhood instead of the *Imago Dei*. Effectively, they replace the *Imago Dei* with the *Imago Homo*.

What is a robot for? In industry, robots and computers are used to complete repetitive tasks or to make calculations with massive data sets much more quickly than a human could. When designed correctly, they do not replace the human function;

---

19   For an extreme example of this, please see Jason Thacker, *The Age of AI* (Zondervan, Grand Rapids, MI, 2020), pg. 82.
20   Simone de Beauvoir, *The Second Sex*, Volume II, translated by Constance Borde and Sheila Malovant-Chevallier (Alfred A. Knopf, NY, NY, 2009), pg 330.

they assist it. It's much faster to have robots construct cars, and it reduces repetitive motion injuries. However, the human still designs the car. A robot is essentially a thing to be used. Our confusion in "making babies" vs. begetting children rears its ugly head again here. Having "made" children, whom we instinctively regard as persons, but backhandedly refer to as things, we reverse the logic to bestow personhood on a thing that we've made, not begotten.

While "social robots" make for interesting cinematic experiments, they are impossible for two reasons. First, the work of philosopher Michael Polyani argues convincingly that there are many truths that can't be put into words. Polyani's paradox states that "we know more than we can tell."[21] This is especially true when someone who is an expert at something tries to teach his craft to someone who knows almost nothing about it. The teacher knows his subject so well that he doesn't think about it, "running on auto-pilot" in the modern vernacular. The paradox has far-reaching implications for robotics. How can a programmer possibly be expected to write code for something that he can't even put into words, much less put into a programming language?

Polyani's paradox is also implicitly contained in such works as *Ex Machina* and *Westworld*. The criteria for both the characters and the audience to sympathize with the robot is "it acts like a person." What exactly does it mean to "act like a person"? Those criteria as such can't be programmed into a computer. This even applies to how we look, a much simpler problem than how we behave. One of the criticisms of the film *Rogue One* was that the digitally rendered characters of Governor Tarkin and Princess Leia didn't quite look like people. It's interesting to note that a subsequent film, *The Rise of Skywalker*, used archive footage of the late Carrie Fisher to play Princess Leia instead of re-attempting to digitally render her.

21   Michael Polanyi, *The Tacit Dimension* (University of Chicago Press, Chicago, Ill, 1966), pg. 4.

The second reason is related to the first. Robots don't have souls. If one of the body's purposes is to mediate the soul, but no soul is there, conversing with a robot is like talking to a recording, essentially interacting with nothing. A common frustration with automated help lines is the desire to "talk to a real person." While one reason is certainly the finite options of the automated system, another is the desire to connect, at least on a limited level, with a person.

Another aspect of "acting like a person" is emotion. Humans are innately emotional creatures. We consider the inability to react to events in an emotionally appropriate manner to be a symptom of mental illness. *Star Trek* explores the necessity of emotion over several series. The most well-known example is Spock, but Seven of Nine and Data are also emotionally stunted for different reasons. (Seven was assimilated by the Borg at a young age and has not developed in a normal manner, while Data is a robot.) Part of the intrigue of such characters is the tension generated as they try to deal with emotions; both their own and other peoples'.[22] Under normal circumstances, we would consider Spock's devotion to emotional suppression and strict logical thinking to be borderline sociopathic. Seven would require significant amounts of mental health treatment merely to function. Data would be a novelty item at parties and little else.

Could a robot fake emotion? I don't think so. That's part of "knowing more than we can tell." A robot might say happy things in a happy manner, but there's something behind it that's missing. We can even detect it in people. The term we use is "sincerity," and it also applies to machines, since they lack the ability to care about anything. What definite criteria do we use to determine sincerity? While body language, facial expressions, and tone of voice certainly play a part, there's something beyond what we can verbalize. Given that the

22 Francis Fukuyama, *Our Posthuman Future* (Picador NY, NY 2003), pg. 169-170.

body's purpose is to mediate the soul and express love towards God and other people, we shouldn't be surprised that robotic attempts at politeness and sincerity unnerve us, like the HAL 9000 from *2001: A Space Odyssey*.

What exactly is intelligence?

An indispensable aspect of the "social robot" dream is artificial intelligence (AI). Without the capacity to gather information from its environment and act on it, the best-looking robot in the world is little better than an expensive paperweight. While *Westworld*'s robot "hosts" are the stuff of fertile imaginations, artificial intelligence is with us right now, often closer to us than we consciously realize. The speed with which Amazon's Alexa, Microsoft's Cortana, and Apple's Siri have embedded themselves in household use is breathtaking.

British mathematician Alan Turing, regarded as one of the founding fathers of the computer and artificial intelligence, proposed a simple test to measure a machine's intelligence. A machine and a human, separated by a curtain, would pass messages between each other. A third party, not participating in the conversation, does not know which one is human or which is the machine, but evaluates the messages to attempt to figure out which is which. If the third party cannot tell the difference, the machine passes Turing's test, and is considered to have some level of intelligence.[23] Put Alexa, Cortana, or Siri behind Turing's screen, and at least two of them might pass his test right now. We're further down the road than we realize.

Artificial intelligence can be a useful tool, especially in industry. The raw data that humanity now generates is mind-boggling. The sheer volume of it, even in a single manufacturing

---

23   This assertion is controversial and has been for decades. For example, John Searle's "Chinese room" thought experiment argues that, while a computer may fool the third party into thinking it's a human, it doesn't really *understand* the conversation, and thus the Turing test omits a crucial part of intelligence.

plant, can be overwhelming, making discernment of any order or pattern in it impossible. Entire industries have arisen to allow manufacturing plants to collect more data from more locations, faster than ever before. Artificial intelligence, with ever-faster processors behind it, uses this data to look for discernible patterns or alert the operators to approaching problems.

Technologies that start in industry move into the home, and artificial intelligence is no different. Residential applications of it can be quite difficult, as the sometimes-humorous results of Google's speech translation site show. However, more and more businesses are interested in artificial intelligence. Facebook uses it to determine what you want to see in your news feed and to try to weed out "fake news." Netflix analyzes your viewing history, compares it to other account histories, and then attempts to figure out what you want to watch next. Banks use it to improve their loan-making decisions. Google and Apple use it to find the faces in our pictures and then group them together.

It's one thing to use artificial intelligence to predict the behavior of a manufacturing process, but now we expect it to do more for us than ever before, in increasingly "softer" applications. For example, one hope for it is that it can eliminate human biases and make decisions merely on data in areas such as hiring, to use one example. The project has a critical flaw: the ones building the model often unwittingly import their unconscious biases into the model, even if only through the data they feed it. Such a model was used for a while until it gave a spectacularly undesirable result, penalizing resumes for using forms of the words "woman" or "female."[24] In another egregious example, one Google AI classified faces of African Americans along with gorillas.[25]

---

24   https://www.reuters.com/article/us-amazon-com-jobs-automation-insight/amazon-scraps-secret-ai-recruiting-tool-that-showed-bias-against-women-idUSKCN1MK08G, last accessed, March 9, 2020.
25   *The Age of AI*, pg 148-149.

This is not a blanket disparagement of artificial intelligence. Like all technology, it is a tool, but it also is showing that we, like our forebears, have not learned from history. We currently look to AI as that thing that will finally allow us to create "systems so perfect that no one will need to be good."[26] This has happened before. The turn of the 20th century was accompanied by unbridled optimism in technological progress, and indeed, it was an era of tremendous progress. Electric power, the automobile, the airplane, and the x-ray machine were a few items invented or mass-produced before 1914. Some of this new technology was put to brutally good use killing soldiers on the battlefields of World War I. Technology won't save us; it will merely assist us in destroying ourselves and others more quickly without God's restraining grace.

What should we do? While ethicists, philosophers, and theologians are grappling with the implications of artificial intelligence on our lives, we should seriously consider how much of it to allow in our homes. We, using our bodies, are still under the creational mandate to take dominion over the earth and steward it as God's vice-regents. Yes, technology and machines help us do that, but it crosses a line when it's designed to do the work for us rather than assist us in doing it.

Certain AI technology, such as Alexa, is designed to reduce the amount of thinking we do. We want it to find movies or music that we might like instead of experimenting on our own or reading reviews. Again, this is an attempt to absolve ourselves of our creational responsibility to engage with art, good, bad, or indifferent. The fact that some of these programs are always listening to everything we say is also problematic at best.

It's easy to dismiss concerns about robotics, cybernetics, or the transgender movement as the reactionary last gasp of a dying way of life at best, or bigoted and misanthropic at worst.

---

26   T.S. Eliot, "Choruses from the Rock," Part VI, Line 23.

Undoubtedly, there are some corners of resistance to these new movements that spring from such motives. However, as C.S. Lewis observed, perceived progress isn't always progress, and if one has gone down the wrong road, the necessary thing to do is turn around and go back the way he came.[27] Unwarranted faith in technology and abandoning our fundamental design is going down the wrong road. Another reason to be wary is that by redefining ourselves as biological machines, we consign ourselves to a machine's fate, namely obsolescence and the scrap heap. This is much more than an insult to our dignity; it is also an invitation to our own deaths. To that, we turn next.

---

27   *Mere Christianity*, pg. 36.

Chapter 7

World Without End

A popular piece of business/management advice states, "Begin with the end in mind." You can't just make up a plan as you go along in business. You must know what you do, why you do it, and most importantly, what your solution will look like when a customer implements it. This also applies to the intermediate steps and the day-to-day operation of business. What is my goal? What do I want this to look like when I'm done?

If smart people do that with respect to earthly things, how much more does God — who ordained the end from the beginning (Isa. 46:8-11) do it with his own affairs? Not only do all things work together for good for those who are the called according to his purpose (Rom. 8:28), but they work together towards a larger pre-determined end.

Christians talk a lot about salvation. My own denomination growing up spoke of being born again (John 3). One time and place where it was always mentioned was at funerals. In the preachers' defense, people at funerals are usually thinking about the afterlife anyway, so it made sense on one level. I've been to more than my share of funerals. I didn't even know many of the deceased. I can count on one hand the number of times that the word "resurrection" was mentioned. Most of the time, there was some sort of gospel presentation, albeit truncated. Sometimes, there was a warning about hell, or an encouragement about heaven. Both these are true, but not the whole story.

Salvation is about our bodies as well as our souls

The rest of the story is that the redemption of our souls necessarily leads to the redemption of our bodies. If we are embodied souls and spiritualized bodies, then what happens to one part of us must ultimately happen to the other. Just as sin in the Garden killed our souls immediately, with our bodies dying later, redemption resurrects our souls, with our bodies resurrecting on the last day.

I have had arguments with professing Christians who insisted that we received new bodies at the final judgement. That is emphatically **not** what orthodox Christianity teaches. Receiving new bodies is called "reincarnation." "Resurrection" means that the bodies we have right now will, in a manner beyond our understanding, be reassembled and restored to life, much fuller life than we experience now, and that our souls will be reunited with our bodies. Our bodies will then be incapable of dying, because they will be preserved forever by the power of God.

So why does this matter? Strangely enough, bad teaching about the resurrection and the afterlife often works its way backwards into the present life, where it wreaks destruction. We see this most prevalently in end-of-life ethics. It's one thing to decide that further medical treatment is futile and opt for palliative care. It's quite another to intentionally hasten death through drugs or withholding food and water. Why would we murder someone like that, especially someone we love? We tell ourselves that this suffering is pointless, and that since Paul judged it better by far to depart and be with Christ (Phil. 1:23), why not just drop this shell and go?[1] While that may be appropriate for some crustaceans, bodies are integral parts of what it means to be human.

If bodies are integral parts of what it means to be human, then caring for them is as important as caring for our souls. While Jesus came to bring redemption, he also healed people and, at least twice, miraculously provided food for thousands of people (Mat. 14:13-21 and 15:32-39). The church, throughout its history, has given out food, founded hospitals, and even charged into epidemics when others ran away. The notions of "quality of life" weren't even considered; the idea of the image of Jesus in the face of the needy was.

How did we get to the point where food and water are considered medical care instead of some of the most basic needs of a person's life? In current American medical thought, if we're not in immediate danger of dying, food and water are considered needs; if we are, it's an unwarranted intervention. The tricky part of this discussion is that there are situations where forcing the body to accept nutrition does more harm than good. In such situations, we should refrain from causing unnecessary distress, recognizing that death has arrived, but **only** if death is imminent.

In my experience, such "shell" logic is most prevalent at funerals. I remember looking at the body of my great-grandmother in her casket and hearing someone say that it wasn't her. The unspoken part of that was that, since her spirit was gone, what made her Stella was gone, and a lump of decaying carbon was all

---

1   Unfortunately, no less a figure than John Calvin states that "the body is a prison" at least three times in the *Institutes of the Christian Religion* (3:6:5, 3:9:4, 4:15:11).

that was left behind. To paraphrase C.S. Lewis, that's mistaking what something is made of for what it is.[2]

Part of what made her Stella was her body. That was the same body that hugged my body. That was the same body that ate Christmas dinner with me and too many of her descendants stuffed into too small of a house. I realize that's stilted language. I would normally write that we hugged each other, and we ate together. However, I say this to point out that these things were done by our bodies. Our spirits weren't directly interacting with each other. They were mediated by our bodies.

Jesus did the same thing by eating with his disciples after he rose from the dead. Peter makes a point that he "ate and drank" (Acts 10:41) with him. Remember that Christ still bears the marks of his crucifixion. He could have just healed them, but they remain, at least in part, to show us that the same body that was buried is the same body that came out of the grave. Radically renovated, but the same.

Thinking more about the world to come

The ultimate problem is that we have an inadequate view of suffering and the afterlife. There's a bad joke about a devout Calvinist who falls down a flight of stairs. After painfully standing up, he rubs his bruises and says to himself, "Well, I'm glad **that's** over." Is that how Christians are to view suffering and death?

Paul again: "... in my flesh, I am filling up what is lacking in Christ's afflictions ..." (Col. 1:24). This is a passage that many Western Protestants stumble over, and not just because of the soteriological interpretations it's undergone through the years. A more fundamental problem is that our practical theology has excised suffering. Throughout most of human history,

2   C.S. Lewis, *The Voyage of the Dawn Treader*, found in *The Chronicles of Narnia* (Harper Collins, NY, NY, 2002), pg. 522.

it was assumed that suffering was a normal part of life, and that suffering forced us to grow and mature as human beings. Strangely enough, Christians in poorer countries have more joy and more robust faith in the face of suffering than we rich Christians do who don't face it nearly as much.

Please note that we are not sadists. Jesus fought against suffering, as did the apostles. Part of how we show our love for our neighbors is to alleviate their suffering where we can, most often by meeting their physical needs.

As Christians, we have something better to offer the world, but how often do we give it? Ask yourself a question. What was the last worship song that you heard, either on the radio or in a worship service, which focused on the glories of heaven or of the fullness of Christ's return? *Joy to the World*, most likely. While we think of it as a Christmas song, it was originally intended as an Advent hymn. Other than that, what other modern song can you immediately name that also focuses on Christ's coming reign and the restoration of the world? Yes, God is great, mighty, loving, and compassionate, but he is also our coming King. Too often, we talk about the abundant life in the here and now. I don't want to downplay the presence of Christ and the power of the Spirit in our lives, but I fear that the world has shamed us into silence about the resurrection. The world may cynically dismiss it as pie-in-the-sky-by-and-by, but, "either there is pie in the sky or there is not."[3] As Christians, we hold that there is.

So if there's pie, how much is there? Paul makes an audacious claim when he says, "For I consider that the sufferings of this present time are not worth comparing with the glory that is to be revealed to us" (Rom. 8:18). Really? Really?! There is something that makes Joni Erickson Tada's fifty years in a wheelchair as a near-quadriplegic look like nothing? There's something that makes war crimes and human trafficking and spousal abuse

3   C.S. Lewis, *The Problem of Pain* (Touchstone, New York, NY, 1996), pg. 129-130.

insignificant? We look at suffering, structural injustice, disease, famine, war, and all the other horrors of the world, and wonder: if God really cares, why doesn't he do something about it?!

He will. That something is the resurrection of the body.

Ressurection — without it, Christianity makes no sense

This is **not** optional. European theological liberals in the 19th and 20th centuries attempted to make religion more palatable to its "cultured despisers," to use theologian Fredrich Schleiermacher's infamous phrase. To do that, they began removing any hint of the supernatural or the miraculous from the faith. That includes the resurrection of Christ himself. The outlandish explanations that they came up with to "de-mythologize" the Bible strain credulity so much that one is reminded of Orwell's admonition that some things are so foolish that only educated people can believe them. That's not new. Some tried it in Paul's day:

> Now if Christ is proclaimed as raised from the dead, how can some of you say that there is no resurrection of the dead? But if there is no resurrection of the dead, then not even Christ has been raised. And if Christ has not been raised, then our preaching is in vain and your faith is in vain. We are even found to be misrepresenting God, because we testified about God that he raised Christ, whom he did not raise if it is true that the dead are not raised. For if the dead are not raised, not even Christ has been raised. And if Christ has not been raised, your faith is futile, and you are still in your sins. (1 Cor. 15:12-17)

Yes, you read that right. No resurrection, no Christian faith (see 1 Cor. 15:19). If there's no bodily resurrection, the apostles are all liars, the New Testament is a sham, and all Christians should either convert to another religion or commit suicide. That's how important it is.

Francis Bacon once posited that "It is as natural to die as to be born,"[4] and many Christians seem to agree with him. This is a lie from hell itself. We need to emphatically remind the world that death is the most unnatural thing that we will ever encounter. Death is the final result of the Edenic curse, the "natural" result of human sin, which is the only thing "natural" about it. Re-read Genesis 3. This isn't the way it's supposed to be.

Jesus never even hinted at such a thing. As a matter of fact, he raises four people from the dead in the Gospels (Mk. 5:21-43; Lk. 7:11-17; John 11; and himself at the end of all four Gospels, see Jn. 10:17-18). In one resurrection account (John 11), Jesus specifically raised Lazarus as a preview of his own resurrection, which itself is a preview of the resurrection of the church at the end of this age. Jesus tells Martha,

> "Your brother will rise again." Martha replied, "Lord, I know that he will rise again in the resurrection on the last day." Jesus said to her, "I am the resurrection and the life. He who believes on me will never die. Do you believe this?" (Jn. 11:23-26)

We need to applaud and emulate Martha's belief in the resurrection. At a surface reading, it sounds like Jesus is throwing out a platitude with "your brother will rise again." (Not really. See 1 Thess. 4:18) When Martha affirms the general resurrection, Jesus reveals to her that resurrection itself is an icon. When he says, "I am the resurrection," he tells her that the

4   Francis Bacon, "Of Death," found in *Essays and New Atlantis* (Walter J. Black, Roslyn, NY, 1942), pg. 9.

body has a meaning that points beyond itself, even in death and through death.

What is that meaning? As before, even though it is broken, the body maintains its nuptial meaning. While death inevitably comes for us all, love doesn't want to submit to it. What resurrection proclaims is that love is stronger than death.[5] Resurrection is the final proclamation that death, decay, and evil, no matter how strong they look or how loudly they roar, will not win in the end.

I hasten to add that physical death is not the worst thing that could happen to a person. When a Christian dies, he goes to be with the Lord immediately, and yes, that's better than staying here in a decaying body that may be in pain or delirious. It's also better to see Christ face to face, and to be free from the power and presence of sin. However, as with marriage, we stop too soon when discussing dying and rising again. Paul has this to say about the intermediate period between a believer's death and his resurrection:

> For we know that if the tent that is our earthly
> home is destroyed, we have a building from God,
> a house not made with hands, eternal in the
> heavens. For in this tent we groan, longing to put
> on our heavenly dwelling, if indeed by putting it
> on we may not be found naked. For while we are
> still in this tent, we groan, being burdened—not
> that we would be unclothed, but that we would
> be further clothed, so that what is mortal may
> be swallowed up by life (2 Cor. 5:1-4).

There's nakedness again! Outside of Eden, nakedness is associated with shame. Is there then implicit shame for the disembodied souls in heaven? No. They are free from the

---

5   Song of Solomon 8:6-7 and *Theology of the Body* pg. 597.

presence and power of sin, and they see Christ face-to-face. There's nothing to be ashamed of, but their current state isn't the Creator's full intent. Notice what Paul says: we don't want to be unclothed, but **further** clothed. Souls without bodies aren't dressed, and souls in perishable bodies aren't fully dressed. In a certain sense, we're all walking around on this earth in our spiritual underwear.

Getting dressed for the wedding

An oft-overlooked passage gives us some insight into this:

> When he opened the fifth seal, I saw under the altar the souls of those who had been slain for the word of God and for the witness they had borne. They cried out with a loud voice, "O Sovereign Lord, holy and true, how long before you will judge and avenge our blood on those who dwell on the earth?" Then they were each given a white robe and told to rest a little longer, until the number of their fellow servants and their brothers should be complete, who were to be killed as they themselves had been. (Rev. 6:9-11)

We must be careful of reading apocalyptic literature too woodenly, so I don't believe that these are ghosts in material robes. However, it is interesting that they are given a covering and told to wait, even though there is no shame for them. So why bother with covering if there's no shame?

The answer is glory.

"Glory" is one of those words like "time:" we know exactly what it is until asked to define it.[6] C.S. Lewis defines it as praise

---

6   St. Augustine, *Confessions*, translated by Albert Outler (Thomas Nelson, Nashville, TN, 1999) , Book 11, Chapter 13.

or good repute.[7] That is reflected by a quote on the USA's Tomb of the Unknown Soldier, which reads, "Here rests in honored glory an American soldier known but to God." However, such praise isn't enough for us. After all, the soldiers in every Tomb of the Unknown Soldier around the world are still dead.

That praise or good repute will be completed on the last day, when Christians will be resurrected to the judgement of vindication. It will be so complete that our bodies, which shared in our condemnation, will share in our vindication. The technical term for it is glorification, fittingly enough. Paul tells us that "this perishable body must put on the imperishable, and this mortal body must put on immortality" (1 Cor. 15:53). It's almost like we really are changing clothes.

This kind of clothing/glory imagery is referenced in at least two places for God himself. Isaiah's temple vision (Isaiah 6) references the train of God's robe filling the temple. This fits with the kingly imagery of the passage. We see such imagery again in Revelation 1 when John sees Christ dressed in a linen tunic and a golden sash around his chest. Again, this is part of the blinding display of Christ's glory.

If there's to be a final wedding between Christ and his church, then there needs to be a final wedding dress. In America, there is a wedding tradition that the groom is not allowed to see his bride's wedding dress until he sees it on her as she walks down the aisle. However, the Apostle John can't help but give us a peek at the church's dress:

> ... for the marriage of the Lamb has come, and his Bride has made herself ready; it was granted her to clothe herself with fine linen, bright and pure"—for the fine linen is the righteous deeds of the saints. (Rev. 19:7b-8)

---

7   C.S. Lewis, *The Weight of Glory*, pg.33.

This imagery is not unique in the scriptures. Exodus 28 and 39 provide exquisite detail on the high priest's garments, which, in addition to covering his nakedness (Ex. 28:42), were also for "glory and beauty" (Ex. 28:2). The undergarments, by covering nakedness, deal with shame, while the ephod, which is the outermost layer, glorifies the priest. Remember Paul's assertion that he would present the church to Christ as holy and spotless? The priest's clothing gives us an ever so small preview of that. God graciously covers the priest's shame and replaces it with glory.

No one on Earth does formal dress like British royalty. From my American point of view, it seems like there's a different outfit for every role in the monarchy for every occasion. While we Americans may not have a wardrobe and fashion rules that extensive, we instinctively realize that different occasions call for different clothes. We wear caps and gowns to high school and college graduations. I've already mentioned weddings. We have formal parties where tuxedos and evening gowns are expected. Why is that? Why can't we show up for any of these events in a tracksuit?

The answer is that our outside reflects our inside. A tracksuit implies that we're preparing for strenuous physical activity. Wedding clothes are culturally appropriate for the joy and solemnity of the occasion. Those are only two examples. Clothing isn't just utilitarian; it points toward the occasion. Just like the body has a meaning, clothes have a meaning.

That's part of why Paul says, "put on immortality" (1 Cor. 15:53). We need to properly dress to live in the restored kingdom. Just like astronauts need spacesuits to survive the rigors of space, our bodies need further clothing to withstand the rigors of the New Heavens and the New Earth.

Our resurrected bodies — different, but the same

A question that comes up sometimes is, "Will we still be male and female in heaven? After all, Paul does teach us that in Christ, 'there is neither...male nor female'..." (Gal. 3:28). Some have argued that this, combined with Jesus's teaching about no marriage in heaven, and by implication, no sexual activity, militates against us being male or female. If we can't use the organs, what's the point of having them?

First, God, unlike the devil, doesn't trash his work or break his tools.[8] A more biblical way to say it would be, "... the gifts and calling of God are irrevocable" (Rom. 11:29). If manhood and womanhood reveal some of the attributes of God, why would God obliterate them? Second, just because we won't use our sex organs for their original purposes doesn't mean that they won't have secondary or maybe even new functions. God is not a utilitarian. He didn't have to make flowers of all different colors, and yet he did. Third, if masculinity and femininity are basic to being human, why dispense with it? When God remakes someone or something, he tends to make it more like itself. He makes it greater, not lesser. It's sin that devolves and debases.

Some have speculated that the sexual function will be replaced with something.[9] What we do know is that we will be with Christ and in Christ. Just as Christ fulfilled the sacrificial system, making sacrifices obsolete, the final marriage between Christ and the church will fulfill every marriage, Christian or not, that went before and pointed to it, making marriage, as we know it now, obsolete.

---

8   Adapted from C.S. Lewis, *That Hideous Strength* (Scribner, NY, NY, 2003), pg. 314.
9   C.S. Lewis, *Miracles*, p. 260-261. Also see Greg Morse, "How Could Heaven Not Have Sex?" found at https://www.desiringgod.org/articles/how-could-heaven-not-have-sex, last accessed June 3, 2019.

Cremation, better described as burning our loved ones to ash

The implications of resurrection also mean that we need to rethink our positions on cremation. Let's call it what it is, burning up our loved ones. Using "cremation" is another example of calling something by a different name to make it more palatable. Many reasons for burning up our loved ones are often given: cheaper, less space, easier on the environment, etc. However, if "the body speaks a language of which it is not the author," doesn't it follow that our bodies continue to speak even in death?

What message might we be sending by burning up our loved ones? By our actions, we're saying that bodies are unimportant. This isn't new. It goes back as far as Plato and has persisted through the church era in one form or another. We unintentionally reinforce this by arguing that the dead body will decay anyway, so it doesn't matter if we accelerate the process. As with contraception, we should not only consider the end, but also the method by which we arrive at the end. Using that logic, if Grandma is about to die anyhow, we should smother her with a pillow and get it over with. Some might object that it's not a fair comparison, but isn't the same utilitarian logic behind both? Aren't both using the brutal logic of efficiency over everything else?

What do we burn? Trash and refuse. Are our bodies trash? No. Jesus himself has a body, and has joined himself to all humanity, in a limited sense, by taking on a body.[10] Just as he was filled with the Spirit, so are we to be. If our bodies are temples of the Holy Spirit (1 Cor. 6:19), then cremation isn't merely the acceleration of a natural process, it's burning a church down while the worshippers are away on summer vacation.[11] It's also worth noting that Hindus and some Buddhists burn their dead.

10   *Gaudium et Spes* 22.
11   David Mills, "Temple of the Holy Spirit" in *Touchstone*, Sept. 2008, pg 21.

Both religions teach reincarnation, and that the goal is to be free of the body and this plane of existence. In both religions, bodies are ultimately unimportant, as is the physical world.

Amazingly, the resurrection of humanity is also linked with that of the cosmos. Just as man's sin introduced death into the world, Romans 8 explicitly links the resurrection of the cosmos with the resurrection of man:

> For the creation waits with eager longing for the revealing of the sons of God. For the creation was subjected to futility, not willingly, but because of him who subjected it, in hope that the creation itself will be set free from its bondage to corruption and obtain the freedom of the glory of the children of God. For we know that the whole creation has been groaning together in the pains of childbirth until now. And not only the creation, but we ourselves, who have the firstfruits of the Spirit, groan inwardly as we wait eagerly for adoption as sons, the redemption of our bodies. (Rom. 8:19-23)

If we are connected to the created order as argued in chapter 2, then this makes sense. When we rebelled, in a certain limited sense, we cut creation off from God. When we are restored, the creation, again, in a limited sense, is restored to its connection to God.

Physics meets theology (Really?)

However, I think that the resurrected cosmos will be a little different physically. A bane of science is something called the second law of thermodynamics. Simply put, it states that you must do work to move heat from something cold to something hot. Seems obvious, yes? The melted ice on the shelf never refreezes unless we put it in the freezer again.

Why is this such a big deal? It basically means that the total disorder of the universe is constantly increasing, and that the amount of available energy to use for re-ordering it is decreasing all the time. Not only can we not get more energy out of a system than we put in, we can't even get back what we put in. If it weren't for this law, power plants could produce 50—100% more power than they do, and cars could easily get 100 miles per gallon. Therefore, every closed physical system — like the known universe — ultimately loses usable energy and inexorably decays to its lowest possible state. All you should do to see the truth of this is to, as Stephen Hawking famously suggested, stop making repairs on your house and observe the results.[12] (With four young children in my house, I see it much more quickly by not vacuuming or sweeping.)

If we're going to live forever as resurrected people in a resurrected universe, this could be a big problem. What's the solution? Get rid of or at least modify the second law. Paul may not have known about the second law, but he knew about the death and decay we all experience, not just in our own bodies, but in the entirety of our experience. Like Paul, I too want a universe "free from bondage to corruption" (Rom. 8:21). If God is not a God of disorder (see 1 Cor. 14:33, NIV), isn't the second law a clue that something's not right with the way things are?

The mysterious thing about this is that certain biological processes simply don't work without the second law functioning as it is. One notable example is cellular diffusion, which is vital in both plant and animal cellular biology. Higher animals (like we humans) also need the heat their bodies generate — a direct result of the second law — to maintain the biochemical processes that keep them alive. Such processes may need to be "reworked"

---

12 Stephen Hawking, *A Brief History of Time* (Bantam Books, NY, NY, 1988), pg. 102.

as well. In addition, God's concept of order undoubtedly differs from a physicist's concept of order.

So will God totally destroy everything, then?

Will this creation be destroyed? Yes and no.[13] As I write this, a small city in the Smoky Mountains near my home was destroyed by a forest fire. Does that mean that the city was totally put out of existence? No. The buildings were destroyed, and people's lives thrown into upheaval, but the mountains and the land still exist. The houses and buildings can be rebuilt, and life can start again, albeit not as it was.

I believe that's what we look forward to on Judgement Day. God promised never to destroy the Earth again with a flood of water (Gen. 9:11), but he said nothing about not raining fire. Granted, God could totally destroy the entire planet, and even the cosmos if he so chose. However, if God trashes this world and makes another one, doesn't that give the Devil a tactical victory? Couldn't the Devil argue that he messed this place up so badly that God had to scrap it and start over?

The resurrection will then bring us full circle. If the world is left as a smoldering ash heap by the wrath and judgement of God (2 Pet. 3:10), then one of our first tasks might be cleanup. We won't need another commission to have dominion over the Earth; we will merely need to properly fulfill it this time. Since we'll already "fill the earth," we won't be multiplying, but we will once again work towards maintaining and increasing the world's order and beauty. Without sin, we'll be much better at it this time.

Not only will the physical world be burned up, human civilization as we know it will be totally destroyed. All previous nations and civilizations will be swept away, subsumed into the one Kingdom of God. We'll also have to go about rebuilding

---

13   My argument here draws from John Piper, *Future Grace* (Multinomah, Sisters, OR, 1995), pg 373-378.

society, as well, if we're to rule and reign with Christ (2 Tim. 2:12). However, this time, civilization will be totally free of all the evil that plagued it before: the haves and the have-nots, inefficient government, cronyism — the list is almost endless.

Aside from masculinity and femininity, what will we be like? Some have misinterpreted Jesus's words here to argue that we will become angels. Not only is that not what he said, but angels are not physical beings and do not have physical bodies.[14] The very word "resurrection" means that people will be incarnated. You can't be resurrected as a spirit being. That's what logicians refer to as a category mistake. That's so far from the truth that it isn't even wrong.

The first implication is that we will have some measure of physicality. After all, if we're going to live in a material world, we must be material ourselves. This is also what the post-resurrection appearances of Jesus should teach us.

The central thread running through this book is that bodies have meaning by design. However, the entrance of sin into the world changed the meaning of our bodies and introduced shame, notably sexual shame. If we are free forever from the presence and even possibility of sin in the resurrection, what implications does this have for meaning?

The meaning will again change. No longer will our bodies mediate our sinful natures, so we will be without shame. However, they won't mediate a marital meaning, either. Why? That icon will now be reality, and we won't need it. Since we will have full communion with Christ, we will then have full communion with each other.

As the regenerate people of God, one of the most pernicious effects of sin is that our bodies and souls fight each other. Paul

---

14   Instances of angels appearing to people in scripture are numerous. If they were incarnate, this was a temporary incarnation, and was not required for spiritual beings to interact with the material world.

speaks of "another law waging war against the law of my mind" (Rom. 7:23). Before the fall, our bodies mediated our souls in original innocence. After the fall, they mediated our sin natures and evoked shame. In the resurrection, not only will there be no shame, our souls and bodies will be integrated on a level not possible in this present age and, it appears, not possible in a pre-fall garden. Paul speaks of this in 1 Corinthians 15 when he writes that, "It is sown a natural body; it is raised a spiritual body" (v. 44).

This does not mean that the body is immaterial. While it is possible that the body may be able, in a manner physically impossible now, to convert into pure energy,[15] this is still material, and not a translation of the physical into a spiritual substance. This means that the body mediates the soul — and is subject to the soul — in a manner that is not now possible. The spirit will still be willing, but the flesh will no longer be weak. That's what Paul means by "spiritual body."

Eastern Orthodoxy speaks of a process called divinization. This is drawn from 2 Peter 1:4, where Peter tells us that we will "become partakers of the divine nature." A common way to phrase it is that "we become by grace what he is by nature." I hasten to add that this is not a variant of Mormonism. We are not little Gods.

I think that we have little concept of the abilities we will have in the resurrection (see Jn. 10:34). If Jesus can appear and disappear at will, why can't we? If the apostles can order death and sickness to flee, reversing the entropy of the universe for a little while,[16] why won't we be able to do the same permanently? Will we be able to do this through our own strength? No. However, if we're filled with the Spirit of God, unable to sin and perfectly

15   This might explain Jesus's ability to appear and disappear at will, or this could just be the overactive imagination of a physics geek who's read too many comic books.

16   "Entropy" describes the physical disorder of a system and is a direct measure of the effects of the second law of thermodynamics.

in tune with his will for the physical creation, we will be able to do it through his power working in us (see Col. 1:29). I suspect that's part of what we're training for in this present life.

The world often spoofs the resurrection and the next life by positing that we all become angels, and all we'll do is sit around on clouds strumming harps forever. "That sounds so interminably boring," they reply. They're right. As an Orthodox priest once encouraged/corrected me, "God's much more creative than that." God makes us more than what we are now. The restored kingdom — literally heaven on earth (see Rev. 21:1-6) — will be more exciting and fulfilling than we can possibly imagine (see Eph. 3:20).

When you're getting ready to be married, it changes everything. My wife had to move her belongings to my house. She spent a good part of the five months between our engagement and the wedding planning it out. I remember that the closer the date got, the more slowly time seemed to move. That last week was almost never-ending. I mention that to remind us that Christ is coming. When he does, it really will be the end of the world as we know it, and it will be the beginning of the world as we can't even imagine. Our bodies now point to a fuller, richer reality then. May God grant us grace to live our entire lives now in the light of the wedding to come.

About the Author

David Tipton is a devoted Christian who makes his living as an engineer. He has studied the *Theology of the Body* as a layman for over a decade. *Made with Meaning* is his first book; it is written, he says, because no one else expressed these points quite the way he felt was needed, when discussing issues of the day in connection with faith.

David writes from Knoxville, Tennessee, where he and his wife, Alison, have five children.

You can reach David at davidtiptontob@gmail.com

CPSIA information can be obtained
at www.ICGtesting.com
Printed in the USA
LVHW090036020921
696505LV00002B/130

9 781954 509047